PRESERVE AMERICA

CARL YOUNG, PhD

Preserve America

Copyright © 2022 Carl Young, PhD
Produced and printed by Stillwater River Publications. All rights reserved. Written and
produced in the United States of America. This book may not be reproduced or sold in any
form without the expressed, written permission of the author(s) and publisher.

Visit our website at *www.StillwaterPress.com* for more information.

First Stillwater River Publications Edition.

ISBN: 978-1-958217-43-6

1 2 3 4 5 6 7 8 9 10
Written by Carl Young, PhD.
Published by Stillwater River Publications, Pawtucket, RI, USA.

Names: Young, Carl, 1941 - author.
Title: Preserve America / Carl Young, PhD.
Description: First Stillwater River Publications edition, | Pawtucket, RI, USA : Stillwater
    River Publications, [2022]
Identifiers: ISBN: 978-1-958217-43-6
Subjects: LCSH: United States. Constitution. | Constitutional law--United States. | United
    States--Politics and government--21st century. | Social problems--Political aspects--
    United States.
Classification: LCC: KF4550 .Y68 2022 | DDC: 342.7302--dc23

My maternal grandmother, Cornea Smith, said,
"Carl, always vote Democrat."

PART 1
CARL'S STORY

I was already incensed over Merrick Garland, just like all Democrats. Charlottesville put me over the edge. I have a Black grandson. Nineteen friends I've had are Jews; half are dead. I wanted my own government. I wrote a constitution and a declaration about our new government. I mailed my declaration to leaders in both parties, asking that it be widely distributed. I picked Hillary Clinton to be my first woman president and Joe Biden to be my first man president.

Stephen Breyer, Ruth Bader Ginsburg, Sonia Sotomayor, and Elana Kagan will become our Preserve America Supreme Court judges. Merrick Garland will be our first nominee. There is no way Republicans could keep Merrick Garland out twice.

I sent off a copy of my constitution to Nancy Pelosi and Chuck Schumer. I asked Nancy Pelosi to let all the Democratic House members know. I asked Chuck Schumer to let all the other Democratic senators know and to announce our new government. I was worried to death about Trump attacking North Korea. On behalf of our new government, I wanted Senator Schumer to ask Joe Biden, Madeleine Albright, and Susan Rice to intervene. I left Hillary Clinton off.

Trump might bomb North Korea just to make his Democratic nem-
eses look bad.

I mailed my letters in January, 2018. In March, I googled "Preserve
America." There is no way on earth I ever thought that neither Nancy
Pelosi's nor Chuck Schumer's staff would read something that had my
return address of "Dr. Carl Young." Dozens of times I have made this
call: "This is Dr. Young the author of Preserve America. Hillary Clinton is going to be our first woman president. Joe Biden is going to be
our first man president. Call me for more information." "This is Dr.
Young. I promised seven Republican attorney generals that I would
save them the trouble and expense of deporting dreamers. Call me for
more information." I called Drew Hammill after I read that he spoke
for Nancy Pelosi. I called the office. No one has ever answered in two
and a half years. Imagine my frustration.

I wrote and called Tom Perez for two months. I emailed Donna
Brazille twice.

I wrote an op-ed to the *Washington Post*. I wrote an op-ed to the
New York Times twice. I wrote Jamelle Bouie at the *New York Times*. I
paid to have a copy hand delivered to Tom Friedman.

I mailed everything to the *Providence Journal*.

I wrote *Time* magazine and made a comment when Nancy Pelosi
was on the cover.

I wrote CNN twice.

"Thank you for contacting the opinion section of the *New York
Times*." I emailed a copy of my press release and later a copy of the
planned Constitution. Neither was published. I looked up the editor in
charge: Stuart A. Thompson. I attached his name and changed my title
from "Democrats can't stand Republicans" to "Democratic politicians
can't stand Republicans. We want our own presidents and Supreme
Court. Pass the bipartisan legislation." Nothing was published.

In June, I mailed a copy of my press release to ten Democrats, six
Republicans, and President Trump. Democrats will forever have a man
and a woman who are president at the same time: Hillary Clinton and

Joe Biden. All my senatorial pairs will have a man and a woman except Rhode Island. I chose Elizabeth Warren because I would vote for her next to Hillary Clinton; Kamala Harris because I am going to have four pairs of Black senators. I wrote my four Rhode Island representatives and senators. Nancy Pelosi and Chuck Schumer because of their positions; Alexandria Occasio-Cortez because I am going to have four sets of Hispanics. I'll have one pair of Native Americans. All elected at large.

In June I mailed my press release and bipartisan legislation to ten of them. I wrote "Goodbye Repubs" on the left hand. In July I called and asked them to hold a press conference and pass the bipartisan legislation. No one read what I had mailed or received my phone message. Here we Democrats are going to have our own everything. It is a mystery.

PART 2
THE PRESERVE AMERICA CONSTITUTION

A PRESERVE AMERICA PROPOSAL THAT NEEDS PASSAGE BY DEMOCRATS AND REPUBLICANS IN HOUSE AND SENATE

I HAVE ATTACHED: HOW TO STOP WAR WITH NORTH KOREA, WHY I THINK TRUMP IS AMORAL, MY ABORTION LETTER TO THE AUSTIN NEWSPAPER, AND WHAT I WROTE ON PUBLIC EDUCATION.

PREAMBLE

I want **Preserve America** to be good stewards of the only earth we are ever going to have. I oppose the America that others like Trump want. I am proud to be a fellow Texan where Lyndon Johnson began Medicare and Medicaid and felt a government should declare war on poverty. I still am. It is mind-boggling that Lyndon Johnson and I grew up in the same state as John Cornyn and Ted Cruz. They just voted for tax cuts for the rich that I think are immoral. I think **Preserve America** should help the average citizen accomplish things and promote the general welfare. They don't. Grandmother asked, "Carl, promise me you'll always vote Democrat because Franklin Delano Roosevelt, a rich man, saved

the country for the poor like our family and all the other poor families."
I still want a government for the poor, working, and middle class.

I just read a review of *The Gifted Generation: When Government was Good* by Daniel Goldfield. I was born in 1941, grew up when "the federal government was the great empire, the great leveler with rules that forced rules of fairness to promote the Constitution's 'general welfare.'" I want **Preserve America** to be that kind of federal government for my kids and grandkids for however long it lasts.

Mom, KKK, Nazis, evil, Charlottesville demonstration, and Trump: My Bowie, Texas history teacher, Mrs. Henry, talked about the Civil War. She said that the Ku Klux Klan marched when she was a child. One pair of shoes was distinctive. It belonged to a deacon in her church. I, having never heard of the KKK, went home and asked Mom. She said they approved of Negros being lynched and mutilated, were evil, and going to hell. It made no difference what anyone else in the church thought. I told my daughter KKK, white supremacists, and Nazis were evil. I think that something is wrong. Republican politicians don't care. I say that is immoral and unethical. Others disagree. I think it is ridiculous to measure how well the citizens are doing by how high the stock market is when politicians own more stock than anyone else I know. My grandkids know little about the KKK. When they do, it won't be in **Preserve America**. I promised myself that I would be vigilant and act against evil never dreaming that my president would embolden them to march in Virginia and say they were some good people.

I have lived in seven states and personally knew a dozen or so bigots before Trump. Now there are millions conned by fear of the bad hombre. No newspaper can do this. No politician can. I am a smart generalist. Much of the time I learn as much from written comments as I do the original. My Constitution begins with the one we have. Additions are necessary but not sufficient. Climate change is so important.

I agree with Trump on two things: he won the lucky sperm lottery and regulations are too expensive and take too much time. We should do thoughtful deregulation.

Preserve America will support Planned Parenthood here and abroad. I'll use developing statistics for African women and children and then repeat them. Voltaire: "Those who can make you believe absurdities can make you do atrocities." Too true: 220 million women want to prevent pregnancies but lack knowledge or do not have access to effective contraception. Melinda Gates is a Catholic. Her church criticized Ms. Gates's contraceptive efforts. Unsafe abortions kill 47,000 women and leave 5 million injured, some permanently.

GiveWell says you can save a life for under $5,000. WHO has many statistics. Immunization costs $300 per life saved. The Stop TB Partnership gives people an extra year from $5 to $50. Diarrhea, treated with a pinch of salt, a cup of sugar, and water.

I think it is cruel and immoral not to have worldwide Planned Parenthood. After climate change and promoting democracy, women were my instant third thought. Planned Parenthood prevents 575,000 unintended pregnancies. How you can oppose contraception and abortion? #MeToo happened after I wrote this. If we make minority women and their children our very first priority, I think the rest will probably do just fine.

Al Gore, past vice president and Nobel Peace Prize winner, author of *The Assault on Reason*: "We are in the midst of a deepening crisis for our democracy... the idea that citizens can govern themselves through rational debate—is in peril. Our democracy depends on a well-informed citizenry and a two-way conversation about ideas, but our public sphere has been degraded by fake news and the politics of fear, partisanship, and blind faith..."

Susan Rice, author of *New York Times* article "To be Great, America Must Be Good": "Trump has wreaked havoc, hobbling our core alliances, jettisoning American values, abdicating United States leadership for the world." She goes on to describe how other countries supported us. I love war movies. I assumed most of the soldiers at Nor-

11

mandy were American. Wrong! Of the 156,000 Allied D-Day troops, 83,000 were English.

Joe Kerry: "Technology, not trade costs 85 percent of 5.6 million manufacturing jobs in the first decade of this century. Need a new plan for investing in the 21st century." He and the rest of us want a plan to invest here and throughout the world. Friedman says we have to prepare for globalization, technology, and climate change.

"Keep America a beacon of progress, stability, and global stewardship."

Preview

I presume to rewrite the Constitution to assure "the general welfare." Here are my main ones: climate, full equality for women, full equality for minorities and LGBTQ, income equality, a health plan that lowers cost, taxation reform, guns, housing, jobs, immigration reform, prison and justice reform, education change, infrastructure, and mandated military and/or public service. The Johnson rule will be in our new **Preserve America** Constitution. So will things I have always thought were wrong but not unlawful. We'll have a new FEMA. Readers can add others.

Who would not want more, better paying, jobs for the lower and middle class? I wish Trump did. The stock market is high.

Aside: I first lived in Archer City, Texas, a bookless town. Uncle Glenn bought me a box of novels in Texas. Mother caught me reading Steinbeck's *In Dubious Battle* in the fifth grade. From then on Mom distrusted fiction, not nonfiction. Bored constantly, I was reading it for the third time and said nothing. I recommend several books by people who are scholars or have important positions. My selections came from the *New York Times* and random finds in my library's nonfiction section. I have included books by people who are scholars and have a position I like.

12

Aside: If you are old and like gospel music, choose Oakridge Boys on Pandora. I would have been a happy Gaither's groupie. Joe & Eddie are on YouTube.

Things you must read and pass in **Preserve America**: our Constitution, civics, American history, world civilization, geography, manners, and ethics. You are expected to be a scholar and learn from a college curriculum like University of Chicago.

Years ago at Penn State, we had a visiting researcher on white-collar crime. One of my graduate students used to be a probation officer in Pittsburg. There was a price-fixing scheme between one Pittsburg CEO and another. Their crime exceeded all the other crime combined. One CEO was found guilty. Instead of going to prison for 20 years, he was given weekly probation. My graduate student would go at the appointed time and be kept waiting for hours. He would then see the crook in a quarter-acre plush office for 15 minutes. White-collar crime is treated just like all the rest of the world wants it!

I assume that when our Congress approves Preserve America, that all the Blue states will vote yes this November 8 to create Preserve America. Huntington's, a hereditary neurological disease, has compromised my fine mind. Preserve America will have two presidents, one woman and one man. The one with the most votes wins.

I am counting these states as Preserve America: California, Colorado, Connecticut, Delaware, Hawaii, Illinois, Maine, Maryland, Massachusetts, Minnesota, Nevada, New Jersey, New Hampshire, New Mexico, New York, Oregon, Rhode Island, Virginia, Vermont, Washington, Georgia, Florida and Washington, DC. I hope every state votes for it. It saddens me that Texas will not be part of it. Washington, DC will have two senators and eight representatives. Puerto Rico will have two senators and one representative.

Preserve America wants to be the world's leader in democracy. I haven't read *Democracy* by Condolezza Rice, the former secretary of state. She gives a sweeping look at the global struggle for democracy and why America must continue to support the cause of human freedom. So must we.

Dan Grant, a friend and mentor, was a political scientist at Vanderbilt. He said if we traded with every nation, wars would cease. Trade tends to be good for everyone. Dr. Grant wrote *The Christian and Politics* and became president of Quachita Baptist College in Arkadelphia, Arkansas.

China worries me. We will have strong leaders who negotiate a new deal with other WTO leaders.

Read Peter Singer's *Ethics in the Real World: 82 Brief Essays on Things That Matter*. I have about as many friends who are atheists as I do Baptist preachers. All of my atheist friends are humanitarians and utilitarian.

The first book I recommend reports what has been happening in Congress for decades. It is by two political scientists. Thomas Mann and Norman Ornstein wrote *It's Even Worse Than it Looks: How the American Constitutional System Collided with the New Politics of Extremism*. They give many examples and conclude that Republicans in their fanatical zeal to recapture Washington were primarily responsible for breaking their congressional branches. There is a serious mismatch between our present constitution's form and what Republicans are doing. The Republican Party is "an insurgent outlier—ideologically extreme, contemptuous of the inherited and social and economic policy regime; scornful of compromise, unpersuaded by conventional understanding of facts, evidence, and science; and dismissive of the legitimacy of its political opposition."

I read Arlie Russell Hochschild's *Strangers in Their Own Land: Anger and Mourning on the American Right*. Some 20 percent of the country might be Tea Party. Louisiana, Mississippi, and other states want no government and take our federal subsidies.

The first policy book I read was Jacob S. Hacker's *American Amnesia: How the War on Government Led Us to Forget What Made America Prosper*. "This book is about an uncomfortable truth. It takes government, lots of government for advanced societies to flourish. This truth is uncomfortable because Americans cherish freedom. Government is effective, in part, because it limits freedom.... Government works because it can make people do things." I read Lee Drutman's "How Corporate Lobbying Conquered American Democracy" in the *Atlantic*. Dozens of books have some form of things-are-hopeless-unless-such-and-such-happens in their titles.

Simon Kuznets said the richest countries have expanded governments. Poorer countries haven't.

Preserve America **taxes**: Beginning January 1, 2023, all the income tax money paid by a Preserve America state will go toward our new government.

We will fund research, science, education, health, arts, and income equality. We think a balance is always needed with the market and government. James Madison said that one purpose of government is to make a man do his duty. Our new laws will reflect that. We want policies that are evidence-based. If that had been President Barack Obama's only contribution, that will now live forever in ours.

Here are ideas and issues for the general welfare. Uncle Glenn said Aunt Ruth did everything like she was killing snakes. The metaphor fits. We can do no less.

CLIMATE

Richard Alley is a glaciologist at Penn State. The Thwaites Glacier in Antarctica is melting. Alley thinks seas will rise three feet in this century. Others predict a rise of **six** feet by 2100. I live on the water. Rhode Island's beaches would disappear at three feet. Hundreds of millions will be displaced at three feet, much less six feet. I read Noam Chomsky's *Requiem for the American Dream*. "We're facing literal questions of species survival. Can the species survive at least in any decent form?" Here is some Republican advice: only pay for repairs that meet a 100-year forecast made by independent planners and engineers.

Preserve America will of course sign the COP21 Paris Agreement. We are willing to be world climate leaders and encourage Republicans to do as much as they can.

GLOBAL WARMING

President Trump, like many Republicans, is totally ignorant about evolution and global warming. His not knowing that Homo sapiens and chimpanzees share 98.5 percent of the same DNA is harmless. His Republican ignorance about global warming is going to destroy the very earth we live on. There is no clean coal. A century ago, our coral reefs were alive and thriving. At today's carbon dioxide level of 400, they are dying. Science is indifferent to politics. In one experiment, at higher carbon dioxide levels, fish lost their ability to detect and respond to predators. An eventual 1,000 carbon dioxide seems inevitable. The last time the world had that level was at the end of the Pleistocene Epoch 3.5 million years ago. All of the global icecaps had melted. Mar-a-Lago and Rhode Island were under hundreds of feet of water. The tropical water temperature was 104 degrees Fahrenheit.

A warming climate is a world issue. We must address it for all children. Six trillion dollars' worth of fuel remains. If all is burned, our temperature will increase 16 degrees Fahrenheit. Global warming is real. The meat I eat should be taxed. Already 20 million face possible famine from global warming. This number will only increase. If everything frozen melted, the seas would rise 160 feet. Hint: Denver stays safe. Denying global warming is nonsense. Dr. Strickland in 1961: "It is not a sin to be ignorant. It is a sin to stay that way."

I am putting Planned Parenthood and LGBTQ in my Constitution. God thinks it is heresy for you to believe that He created them just so some Republicans would have someone to hate. God thought the divine story of David and Jonathan loving each other passionately would have been enough. "Call nothing I have made unclean." David was the one most like God's own heart.

We have technology I never dreamed about. **Preserve America** will fund technological solutions to climate change. We will begin competing with China. Money is freed up for the small businesses. Dad was an eighth-grade roughneck. I was born in an oil field. I own coal reserves. We will fund research and technology that is both profitable and for the general good. Dad said, "Carl, there is many an honest man who never had a chance to steal a million dollars." Make that a billion.

Aside: Here is a Kurt Vonnegut rule that would change politics: "No person is allowed to hold any office that has not read one book, not assigned to him or her." A favorite Vonnegut quote: "I was my character's God. I gave him a life altogether common: a life not worth living and an iron will to live."

TAXES

Blues will have a sweeping comprehensive tax overhaul. I can't get over the fundamental unfairness of our tax code and its complexity (4 million words). Remember the trillions already spent on lobbyists. What they call "business as usual," I was taught was corruption; i.e., trying to protect corporations and businesses from paying more taxes. Pharmaceuticals had 1,400 lobbyists in 2014. (Please don't let my parents know I am a pharmaceutical lobbyist. They think I am a pianist in a whorehouse.) Read T.R. Reid's *A Fine Mess: A Global Quest for a Simpler, Fairer, and More Efficient Tax System*. Read Thomas Piketty's *The Economics of Inequality*. There must be dozens of books on fundamental inequality. I read these two. I just bought David Cay Johnston's *Perfectly Legal: The Covert Campaign to Rig Our Tax System to Benefit the Super Rich—and Cheat Everyone Else*. Unfair taxes drive everyone crazy.

Preserve America's Constitution will support the average person. Alieza Durana wrote the hidden ways that the tax code hurts women. I bought Mimi Abramovitz's and Sandra Morgen's *Taxes Are a Woman's Issue: Reframing the Debate*. I volunteer Madeleina Albright, Alieza Durana, Thomas Piketty, and David Cay Johnston,

Mimi Abramovitz, and Sandra Morgen to be on our tax force. Others should include a single mother with two kids, a blue-collar man, and a sampling of average Americans. My birth certificate says, "Father's occupation: rough neck."

I treated a man who worked for the IRS twice. He talked about the multiples that IRS could bring for every dollar spent on it. **Preserve America** will staff with as many professionals as we need, and go after it.

I would have left the rest of the **Preserve America** tax section blank except that seemed cowardly for someone who has read as much as I have. Here is my starter position to discuss and debate. There will be no individual tax deductions except for education, medical expenses, elder care, children, and others to be publicly discussed. There will be child credits. Why do we protect seniors and not children?

There will be no corporate tax loopholes or tax credits. We go to a 15 percent Value-Added Tax (VAT) on everything. Even illegal immigrants buy things. All online purchases are taxed. There is no final export tax. We will offset the VAT's being regressive by giving the poorest a transparent subsidy, not a tax break. I don't know what it should be. Other taxpayers under the median are taxed at 5 percent. We tax the top 1 percent at 50 percent. I don't know what the tax brackets should be for those above the median to the 99th percentile. Homeowners and renters should both get tax breaks, or neither should. We address child poverty. Preserve America will have open meetings to discuss them.

We tax estates above $5 million for individuals and $10 million for couples at 70 percent with no legal loopholes. Six Walmart heirs have as much money as the bottom 30 percent combined. We are on our way to wealthy inherited oligarchs. Enjoy your billions for a few years and then give them away like the Gates. I don't know what capital gains should be. Treasury estimated years ago corporations and individuals would have savings with a VAT. Think tanks will do the 2020 numbers. Corporations and the top 1 percent should have no loopholes. Tax corporations on the full basis of the profits they derive from their sales regardless of where their production originated. Corporate wealth is taxed no matter where it is. We have too many tax injustices. Some people produce wealth. Other people have become wealthy by taking that money from you and me. There will be as many women as men who work on taxes. Trump won the lucky sperm lottery.

I am naming our tax simplification the "Nina Olson Plan." The VAT has been called the "least-worst tax." I agree. **Preserve America** will promote justice and save lives. Caterpillar, Apple, Microsoft, Google, Amazon, and many others have used quasi-legal/phony tax inversions that look and smell just like what they are. If **Preserve America** laws cannot manage them, our new Constitution will. They will now be criminal. Remove safe harbors. Remember: no deductions, no exceptions. Joseph Stigletz recommends a pollution tax, auctioning oil, gas, and minerals. Subsidies end.

Productivity increased six times. Wages didn't. We stop predatory lending and challenge abusive credit cards. We have subsidized banks. We'll stop "derivatives" and other terms that now work against the middle class and the poor. Name one middle-class person who benefitted from trickle-down economics. We add financial activities taxes. You are taxed on profits whether you bring them here or not. We have laws and regulations that are not enforced. You and I have allowed one set of rules for the rich and another set for all the rest.

Eighty percent of Japanese are mailed their tax information on a postcard. Japanese taxes are deposited in one's bank account or funds are withdrawn. In the UK, one in five have to file. Right now 2.6 trillion tax dollars are overseas and not paid. We want Broad Base Lower Rate (BBLR). We now spend 1 billion hours and $10 billion on tax preparation. That goes to minutes for most individuals. We have deductions on interest of $1 trillion. No more. When a lobbyist wants a loophole: "Sorry, we don't do that anymore. We cannot speak for Republicans. They may." If you feel that sorry about H&R Block, send them a check. Special interests, don't even ask. The answer is no.

The IRS will send you a form with all of your available information on it. You check it, sign it, and mail it in. That's it. I speak for the small taxpayer like me. Our Constitution will no longer permit unlimited anonymous corporate gifts to political candidates. In my lifetime, there have been trillions of federal subsidies and tax breaks to Fortune 500 companies. Fifty-five percent of large corporations paid no federal tax at least one year in one five-year span. Our new Constitution will prohibit treating corporations as individuals.

Remember my high school mom and roughneck dad? First, 47 percent pay essentially no taxes—often for things not their fault. Of course, they should work. Maybe they were waiting for a living wage. Others will figure out their subsidy. Second, some 53 percent of the people can't cover a $400 emergency. We could reduce the loan penalty for those with a 401K to no penalty. We could ourselves become a 3 percent same-day paycheck loan agency or 6 percent credit card. Payday loan sharks can be 500 percent. There should be no usury or avarice.

Aside: We are on our way to an ugly society of fear and hatred. Douglas Fraser: "We now have multinational corporations that know neither patriotism nor morality, only self-interest." We will balance private gain and social benefit.

INFRASTRUCTURE

Something like $1.5 trillion is needed. Uncle Glenn Smith spent his life in oil and thought gasoline should be taxed an additional dollar. A semi used to do the road damage of 8,000 cars. My family had two truck drivers. I support their subsidy.

HEALTH INSURANCE

I was principal vice president at Blue Cross and Blue Shield of Rhode Island. I used to be a health expert. In 1993 Blue Cross plans had a Medical Loss Ratio (MLR) of 95. Texas Blue Cross Blue Shield in 2014 had 64.4. **Preserve America** will lower the cost of health insurance. Elizabeth Rosenthal will lead our initiative; Irene Papanicolas, Liana Workie, and Ashish Jha will work with her. We want them to develop, and for the whole nation to use, our drug benefit. I cannot imagine any economic plan that will help my friends and family more. I bought two copies of Elizabeth Rosenthal's *An American Sickness: How Healthcare Became Big Business and How You Can Take It Back.* She, our politicians, and other health experts won't stop until **Preserve America** gets our new plan in place. All healthcare providers and hospital overhead will go down. Insurance hassle ends. Its costs end. One reviewer of Rosenthal's book named a dozen others. Identify yourselves. If you are in the health system and merging to increase costs, that's immoral. If your private insurer got a billion-dollar bonus, that's immoral. Insurers should be nonprofit just the way Blue Cross used to be. It will be unlawful to make profits off of healthcare.

"It's the Prices, Stupid" was published in *Health Affairs* in 2003, written by Princeton University Health Economist Uwe Reinhardt, along with Gerald Anderson, Peter Hussey, and Varduhi Petrosyan. Americans use about the same amount of healthcare as other countries, but pay a lot more for it. "The only place we stand out is in price." New Jersey will vote for **Preserve America**. I happily volunteer them to be on our health policy planning, pricing, and measurement task force.

Our new **Preserve America** Constitution will specify that the **Preserve America** government has the authority to determine all health professional fees and drug costs if necessary. Physicians who want to go quality will support fee capping. Great.

Rosenthal has written an expert health book. Read it. Be revolted. Health is a $3 trillion business plus the billions that your insurance costs. One in nine works in healthcare. For every physician, there are 16 other health professionals. Half of them are administrative. The US spends $631 per man, woman, and child on administration. Japan spends $54. Millions will lose their jobs. We will have comprehensive job training for everyone. Besides, there will always be jobs for those willing to jack Republican coastal homes up that should have never been built in the first place. We shall offer to retrain everyone who loses a job because of technology and globalization.

If a private insurer won't insure homes and businesses, you have to self-insure. There is no more federal flood insurance subsidy.

Pharmaceuticals and specialists cost us billions. I do this for retirees. Wendy Connick at Motley Fool: "It takes $740,000 to retire. $260,000 of this is the cost of health." A million of us could discuss healthcare for days.

The Congressional Budget Office (CBO) found in 2004 that administrative costs under the public Medicare plan were less than 2 percent of expenditures, compared with approximately 11 percent of spending by private plans under Medicare Advantage. This was a nearly perfect "apples to apples" comparison. It gives me fits to learn that a drug that once cost $1.00 now costs $100. Andy Slavit: "When you take on pharma, you take on this whole town." We have been duly warned. After Congress votes that states can vote for **Preserve America** and your state doesn't, you still get our drug benefit. We become the insurer or reinsurer of last resort, like Blue Cross used to be.

The General Accounting Office (GAO) found that in 2006 Medicare Advantage plans spent 83.3 percent of their revenue on medical expenses, with 10.1 percent going to non-medical expenses and 6.6 percent to profits—a 16.7 percent administrative share. An 83.3 Medical Loss Ratio. One in six US dollars goes for health care. It will be twice that by 2035. Right now 27 percent of Medicare goes to the last year of a senior's death. Ours shouldn't. WHO saves many world lives for $5,000; immunizations save lives at $300 or less.

Of the $3 trillion—physicians are 20 to 30 percent; hospitals, 40 to 50 percent; drug and medical devices, 15 percent; and tests and ancillaries, 20 to 30 percent. We will ban all drug advertising just like Europe does. We go transparent and evidence-based. Our pharmacists should prescribe some drugs just like other countries do. Sixty-two percent of all bankruptcies were because of health. We cover all mental health and alcohol/drug treatment. Depression costs us a fortune in lost labor and misery. I take two medicines for my depression. Psycho-therapy works. Use ours freely. We declare war on opioids with money, not talk. We will pay mental health providers more.

"Putting profits above healthcare is unfair, barbaric, and immoral." Carl, did you know there were Catholic and other for-profit hospitals? No, I did not.

We will build new medical schools and want to support as wide a variety of medical education as we can. We want our students to represent our population.

HIPAA ends. I know public and confidential deaths that occurred because of HIPAA. No one was warned. Do you know any lives that were saved by HIPAA? I don't.

INCOME INEQUALITY

The gap between the rich and everyone else has been growing markedly, by every major statistical measure, for at least 30 years.

Read this book first about income inequality: Joseph E. Stiglitz's *The Price of Inequality: How Today's Divided Society Endangers Our Future*. He won the Nobel Prize in economics. Some things are straightforward. Others aren't. Don't even think about being a **Preserve America** politician without studying income inequality. I bought and skimmed Ganesch Sitaraman's *The Crisis of the Middle-Class Constitution: Why Economic Inequality Threatens Our Republic*. Read a review, if not the whole book.

Just prior to President Obama's 2014 State of the Union Address, media reported that the top wealthiest 1 percent possess 40 percent of the nation's wealth; the bottom 80 percent own 7 percent. Similarly, but later, the media reported, the "richest 1 percent in the United States now own more additional income than the bottom **90 percent**."

10 percent of us own 80 percent of the stock.

59 percent of the workforce is hourly.

3.2 million live on less than $1.50 a day.

5.3 million are absolutely poor.

Let me put this into perspective. If the US had the same income distribution it had in 1979, each family in the bottom 80 percent of the income distribution would have $11,000 more per year in income on average. Our new tax system should bring you more total money. Our **Preserve America** politicians will decide how much. Half of the US population lives in poverty or is low-income. $22,000 for a family of 4 is poverty. See Thomas Piketty's *The Economics of Inequality*. Cutting taxes to 15 percent for the rich does nothing for the middle class. The middle class has shrunk.

Yale Nobel prize winner for economics Robert J. Shiller called rising economic inequality "the most important problem that we are facing now." "This is not the type of thing which a democratic society – a capitalist democratic society – can really accept without addressing." President Barack Obama called the income gap the "defining challenge of our time." Yet he did nothing.

We start to address income inequality. I have not read Lawrence Lessig, *Republic Lost: How Money Corrupts Congress—and a Plan to Stop It*; Larry Bartel, *Unequal Democracy: The Political Economy of the New Gilded Age*; or Nolan McCarty, *Polarized America: the Dance of Ideology and Unequal Riches*. Two more significant publications: *Plutocrats: The Rise of the New Global Super-Rich and the Fall of Everyone Else* by Chrystia Freeland; *Nickel and Dimed* by Barbara Ehrenreich. Ehrenreich tried to live on low-wage jobs and found it was nearly impossible. Interview her and all the other income inequality experts for more detailed information.

EDUCATION

We shall focus on age 3 through college age. What kids learn in public school has been declining since 1963. No one in my lifetime has been dumber than today's students. Distraction by TV started it. Texting is its own nightmare. PEW: "If your child is awake, he or she is distracted." Many employers cannot get adequately educated workers. For-profit colleges have to be reviewed to see if they are legitimate or a scam. See the report on the history of the for-profit colleges by Century Foundation. Three grandkids go to regular public school. I am opposed to government subsidy of religious schools. I was surprised to learn that students with vouchers did worse on math and English than those who did not get one: 33 percent are proficient in math, 40 percent are proficient in English.

I read Ronald A. Wolk's *Wasting Minds: Why Our Education System Is Failing and What We Can Do About It* twice. Education is the key to economic growth, poverty, moving from lower to middle class. The cost of a college education increased two and a half times while inflation was 20 percent. That's outrageous. Boycott them. Tuition at Texas was $54 a semester in 1960. My private college was $15 an hour with a 16-credit cap. Colleges and universities cost 1,000 percent more than in 1978. That has to stop. Linda McNeill and I were in the same house church. She was chair of education at Rice just like Howard Gardner was at Harvard. I want to use Howard Gardner's education process and other content. I volunteer Linda and Gardner as experts to develop and assess education.

BARACK OBAMA

His evidence-based policymaking is a legacy that can never be taken away. We'll use it exclusively everywhere. Public education itself is the single most important. Evidence-based policy is what we use.

Aside: I used to put a number behind an article for how many times my students needed to read it. When asked why I had no "one," I said, "Here is a hard question if you read something just once: Did I read the article or not?"

Aside: I would like to thank the person who taught me "counterintuitive." One thinks one thing is true, and just the exact opposite is true. Vouchers are clearly one. I know kids who will always be sickly because their mother covered everything in

Lysol. They had no natural germ resistance. Some work rules are. Welfare rules broke up families. Those families will never come together again. Do you think a Mexican wall will slow immigration? Two-thirds overstayed their temporary visa.

Aside: I wrote an article on education and special education that was never published. I cite statistics and reference books. I graduated from George Peabody College for Teachers. I am most concerned about public education. Here are my college freshmen's chemistry grades for 15 students: one A, one B, one C, one D, and eleven F's. "Eleven students now know what all lab work is required means."

JOBS

Eighteen of my 88 classmates graduated from college. Eighty percent did just fine without one. I think we need jobs for the two-thirds today who aren't college graduates. Joan Williams wrote *White Working Class*. "We have a dearth of workers qualified for middle-skill jobs that pay $40,000 or more a year and require postsecondary education but not a college degree...a lack of adequate talent affects the productivity of 47 percent of manufacturing companies, 35 percent of health care and social assistance companies. Middle-skill jobs are important jobs: emergency medical technician, electrician, robot-heavy factory worker, wind-turbine technician, and plumbers." If we can afford it, adopt a mandatory two-year commitment to provide wide scale training for military, social services, and other jobs. Federal government job subsidies are a good idea. Right now 9.5 million men (24 to 55) are unemployed some time. Right now 7.2 million are NILF (Not In the Labor Force). They don't want to work and never have worked. David Brooks wrote "The Worker's Paradise"—work that Congress could have passed.

HOUSING

Roughly 1.5 million homeowners broke even on their homes, and 3.2 million homeowners nationally still owe more on their mortgages than their homes are currently worth. Others will work on our housing policy. Alex F. Schwartz's *Housing Policy in the United States: An Introduction* arrived. Like most community psychologists, housing should have been socialist. It should remain affordable, no matter what. A three-bedroom house should cost no more than $200,000 anywhere. What a debt we are leaving our children for housing and for tuition loans. I am a fair housing fanatic. We'll have rigorous laws and legal enforcement.

CRIMINAL JUSTICE AND PRISONS

We shall reform ours. We don't think even more people should be convicted like Jess Sessions. **Preserve America** believes that the goal of criminal justice should be returning people back into society. We want the bare minimum, not starting with the maximum deterrent. Released prisoners should vote. No nation has as many prisoners as we do. Look it up. **Preserve America** will begin justice reform and won't stop until we get it. Prison is the new Jim Crow. We end the death penalty. We redefine ours the way some European countries have. Read *Unfair: The New Science of Criminal Justice* by Adam Benforado. I have Michelle Alexander's *The New Jim Crow: Mass Incarceration in the Age of Colorblindness*. Red states are reforming justice because of its cost. I want it because it is humane. No one should be in jail because they can't pay bail or did some piece of nonsense on probation or parole. Why not have clean slates for prisoners? Many European countries do.

In the early seventies, 200,000 were imprisoned. In 2009, it was 1.6 million. Four states have decreased the number by 20 percent: California, New Jersey, New York, and Rhode Island. We intend to go back to lower than 200,000. Fewer things will be felonies. We'll change bail, and reduce prison sentences for nonviolent offenders. Mandatory public service will provide a transition out of prison and assist probation and parole. Half are nonviolent.

Stan Van Gundy in *Time* Reforms: ameliorate harsh sentences, enact clean-slate laws, eliminate cash bail, reform juvenile justice, end police brutality and bias. Actual annual cost for the US government to hold people in jail on bond—$14 billion. Number of people who have been sentenced to life without parole for crimes they committed as juveniles—2,100. Percentage who are people of color—67 percent.

Aside: Ted Vallance, a friend and psychologist, was my associate dean at Penn State. He studied and wrote a book in retirement on drugs. He ended up thinking drugs should be legalized based on age. Users and abusers should be treated, not imprisoned. I agree. Marijuana legalization should have been approved years ago with a recommended minimum age of 25 years old to sell it to. That will mean nothing.

CONSTITUTION

Republicans have used a wrecking ball on the Constitution they openly swear to uphold and then violate. "If you review Obama's nominee, the Tea Party and Bannon will go after your seat." **Preserve America** starts with our current Constitution and clarifies ambiguities. We will have meetings among scholars and citizens to compose our new Constitution. We will examine issues as carefully as our forefathers did. We will clarify guns, reproductive rights, abortion, increase the power and protection of the press, open disclosure, conflicts of interest, etc. Ours will permit drug, hospital, physician, and practitioner pricing. Ours will include the Equal Rights Amendment. We want transparency. All of us will need to be educated about our new Constitution. Ours will promote income equality and clarify taxation. Experts have thought about state constitutions. Our new Constitution needs additions not subtractions. We need clarification. Some things are obvious. Others will require study. We still believe in civil liberties. New Supreme Court judges are required for our new Constitution. We will enforce. You may know other needed protections.

LGBTQ

Our Constitution will specify your full rights with no qualifications.

Aside: We redo patents. Amazon's patented "one click." Some major players spend more money on lawsuits than R&D. No more nonsense like that. The Court just ruled that if you bought the cartridge you can have it refilled. Here is a story about an HP printer, 15 years ago. I bought extra color cartridges that I did not use for months. When I used them, I found they had a built-in timer. $120 had expired. Outrageous. Why can't I buy a universal cartridge, cord, whatever?

Guns

We shall have reasonable gun laws. Only kooks think AK-47s and armor-piercing bullets were implied in the Second Amendment. Here is a law. It forbids anyone mentioning to parents that guns kill kids. My daughter's job is to prevent violence to children. She was horrified. So was I. If you are a parent with guns and don't protect your children, you are an idiot no matter what the National Rifle Association wants. Parents will develop our gun policies. No, we shall not permit open gun carry and other things. Our new Constitution will clarify our gun policy. Florida has a law that physicians can't discuss that guns are dangerous. It was just overruled. Obama wanted to keep people who were mentally ill from buying guns. President Trump issued an executive order to stop it. I had a psychotic patient who heard voices telling her to shoot two people whom she named. She was unarmed. I called the police. They appreciated my warning and gave her name to local gun dealers. She moved out of state. I own guns and no longer hunt. A Texas childhood dream was to retire and own a gun shop, hunt quail, serve coffee, and swap hunting and fishing stories with other old men. There used to be 30 million quail in North Texas. Now there are only 3 million. That is sad for the hunter and even sadder for the quail.

Immigration

We will have major immigration reform. First- or second-generation immigrants built 200 of the 500 Fortune. Roughly 15,000 US physicians are from the seven Muslim countries that our president first banned. Immigrant physicians practice in our rural areas. One may have treated you. Tech companies, America is back in business. Welcome all technical immigrants back. We'll make them citizens.

We could use colleges as immigration filters for undergraduates and graduates. We will have a policy to make current immigrants legal. We will still deport criminals and people at high risk of violence. We need the right immigrants economically.

Dreamers and Salvadorans are instantly made citizens. It is the ethical and American thing to do.

Immigration policy is complicated. George Borjas wrote "The Immigration Debate We Need" in the *New York Times*. Others wrote informed objections/responses. He and others will be resources. He takes on some common myths. Low-income workers, Blacks, and Hispanics have lost some 6 percent of their earnings over 30 years.

Dad was shot and stabbed for renting to a Mexican family in Bowie, Texas. Can you imagine Senator Cruz feeling that strongly about what is right, to risk his life for a Mexican family? The very idea is absurd. I am proud of New York City and its role in handling so many immigrants. I am proud of California, New Mexico, Washington, and Arizona for their role in immigration. In Houston, 145 languages are spoken. Here is something all native Texans learn: If General Santa Anna with 5,000 soldiers had not been so world-class incompetent, Trump would be building his wall on the Red River between Oklahoma and Texas, not on the Rio Grande.

One of the first things I wanted to see on my high school senior trip was the Statue of Liberty. My heart still swells with patriotic pride when I see it. Preserve America will be happy to keep the symbol of the Statue of Liberty. Neil Diamond's "Coming to America" is on my playlist. Keeping current immigrants is one policy. Who should be admitted is another. We'll work it out publicly together.

Abortions

We would make abortions legal and safe. We would love to have women use contraception so that abortions become rare. A three-year intrauterine device (IUD) with all the appropriate warnings should be used. Two drugs do it. I recognize its moral importance to many. I was reared believing in the separation of church and state. We acknowledge that many are as strongly opposed to abortions, as we are prochoice. Our new Preserve America Constitution will clarify reproductive rights.

Google said 700,000 people searched for "abortion" in 2016. How can one be opposed to both abortion and contraception? That's immoral. Worldwide, 47,000 die from self-induced abortions. Five million women were injured. Conservative Supreme Court justices scare me on abortion. Right now 220 million women want to prevent pregnancies. There are 3 million baby deaths in the first year of life. Right now 9.7 million children under age five die. Like Peter Singer and most ethicists, I am a utilitarian. Anyone opposed to contraception does not care about any of these deaths and medical disasters. We need male contraceptives.

Abortion Clinics

Of course you can protest but no more harassment. Thirty yards away there will be a barrier for you to stand behind. Two signs will be provided. Most of yours will say, "If I were pregnant, I would not have an abortion. If you are pregnant, I wish you would not have an abortion either. I just wanted you to know. It is no longer any of my business." Nuns will have one that reads, "If I had been raped even if by a priest, I would have reported that man to the police and kept the baby." November 2017 the *New York Times* had a long edition about Tuam and other Ireland sites run by nuns. At Tuam almost 950 children's bones were found, from infants to four-year-olds in a home managed by nuns. They had been either starved or killed. At another Irish site another 500 bones were found. Some infant and children deaths around places inhabited by nuns are urban legends. Some have been documented. It is a rare excavation that does not turn up some throughout the world. Most nuns are prolife. Across time hundreds, maybe thousands obviously were not prolife.

PLANNED PARENTHOOD

We want every state to have Planned Parenthood and will fund overseas ventures as well. We want to prevent unwanted pregnancies through contraceptives everywhere. I want Global Aid Health Empowerment.

FOREIGN AID

We believe in it for moral and selfish reasons. A measly 22 cents a day worldwide can reduce poverty. (Direct pay.) We believe in foreign aid. I am reading Peter Singer's *The Life You Can Save*. Right now 1 percent of our GDP goes there. I want 3 percent.

EPA

We strengthen ours. Every clean policy is back on the books.

EQUAL RIGHTS AMENDMENT (ERA)

Full equality will be in our Constitution. Some women oppose the ERA for reasons I'll never understand. It is a woman's onus, if opposed, to say she does not want it. Need persuasion? Here is one depressing book I'll never finish: Susan Faludi's *Backlash: The Undeclared War Against American Women*.

RACE

After the 2008 crash, whites had 20 times more wealth than Blacks. We will have full equality. Dad's dad told him at 13 he no longer had enough food. Dad was 16 and asleep on a moving flatbed train car. He rolled off the end to his certain death. A Black grabbed him by the belt and pulled him to safety. Dad: "I'll always do right by your people."

And so he/we did. Mother had a picture of Willie Mays stuck into the corner of her mirror. I grew up in a white small town in Texas. I integrated my Baptist College when it occurred to me that all the Blacks were males from Africa, not men and women from America. Two Baptist board members were segregationists. I threatened publicity by Bill Jones in the *Fort Worth Star-Telegram*. Howard Payne integrated with two abstentions. I went to graduate school in Nashville where Tennessee State, Fisk, and Meharry were located. I did voter registration and other civil rights stuff. A petite Black girl from Mississippi had the highest IQ on the Stanford Binet to my knowledge. She was in our Peabody gifted program. Her father took her back home to pick cotton over our many pleas and objections. Now I have a Black grandson, whom I worry about. I am pretty intelligent for a white man but not so smart as Easy Rawlings.

Peabody was my first college with Black students. A guy told how he and his family could never drive anywhere without some white person giving them a hateful look, even in Nashville. It was inconceivable that someone hated them just because they were black. Center for Community Studies (CCS) was a "town and gown" organization of faculty and students from Fisk, Meharry, Peabody, and Vanderbilt. Irene Wood, our wonderful immigrant from Scotland, got a higher paying job than our grant covered. Our next secretary did something so that Bob Newbrough had to let them go that same day. Bob, the CCS director, called around. A Meharry faculty member said that one of his new medical students had a wife who was bored. They were well off. She would be happy to volunteer. She was gorgeous and delightful. I came out and found she had a migraine, vertigo, and was almost writhing in pain. I have vertigo myself and offered to drive her home. She was about to have her husband paged at Meharry and come get her. I said it would be quicker if I drove her. She had her husband paged and asked him to meet her at home. Her Mercedes SL convertible already had the top down. I drove her home not thinking anymore about it. I was two years older. We could have been dating. I never saw a Black/

white couple in Nashville and wouldn't see others until Columbia, Maryland. I was driving a gorgeous black woman in obvious pain. I'll never forget the hateful looks that everyone gave me, especially the men. It made a lasting impression. Let's reduce income inequality and discrimination. Many Blacks know how to take this on. We shall.

COURTS

We will have our own Preserve America Supreme Court. We appoint all our own judges. You would have your own. We will take rape seriously. Few men out of a thousand accused rapists enter the justice system. A smaller number get convicted. Maybe 15 to 17 serve time. We oppose all domestic and campus violence. A recent survey from the University of Texas in Austin said 15 percent of female undergraduates said they've been raped while attending there. What a horror. I repeat an earlier caution. Even as I write, Trump is stacking the courts. If Trump appointed you and you are likely to end up in Preserve America get reappointed. I read that Franklin Delano Roosevelt tried to stack the court but couldn't.

I am still indignant that Barack Obama's appointment of Merrick Garland, a moderate, to replace Antonin Scalia was never even considered by the Senate. Senator McConnell and other senators shamelessly stole Judge Garland's position. Had Hillary Clinton won, most Republican senators wanted to keep the ninth Supreme Judge open. I know many thoughtful justice experts. What kind of Constitution and Supreme Court do we want? Don't rush it. Let's openly discuss and debate till we reach an informed comfortable level.

Our Supreme Court will be educated and thoughtful. We shall have a stronger Constitution. Ketanji Brown Jackson, Sonia Sotomayor, and Elana Kagan will become our judges on 1.1.22. Merrick Garland will be our first nominee.

IMMUNIZATIONS

Parents have to immunize their kids. You could let each parent decide. Our immunized kids aren't going to get something when they travel through your Red states anyway. People opposed to immunizations are antiscientific.

BANKS

I have this quaint notion that banks should be banks. "You can bank on it." Otherwise, we don't need them. We would regulate. Never underestimate the power of greed. Many of Trump's banker friends were predators. We welcome whistleblowers. Blues approve thoughtful deregulation. Dodd-Frank was long. Laws should be understandable. The trillions of dollars overseas could act like venture capital until returned.

There is a cycle where the people who are supposed to be regulated write their own. Former government later work as staff or consultants for the same companies they once regulated. No wonder it doesn't work. That self-serving process ends. Let's redo our Federal Reserve Board to represent more public interests. Janet Yellen, you may need to do double duty. No one has impressed me more. Please lead our Federal Reserve planning.

VOTING

One out of four adults are not registered to vote. We promote registration. Like Australia, we shall have mandatory voting. Someone else will figure out whether it should be carrot or stick. No you don't need any ID. Please vote.

MINIMUM WAGE

No one can live on $7.25 an hour. Most folks can't live on the $10 an hour Trump promised. Our starting wage will be $15 an hour for adults and $10 for teenagers. Mostly I was paid a dollar an hour in high school. I made the federal minimum wage of $2.12/hour in the post office in 1959. I could have lived on $2.12, married, bought a small house in Bowie, Texas. My parents bought me a '54 Chrysler New Yorker for $500. That would be $17 an hour today. Of course, I couldn't live on $17 an hour in Rhode Island. We will have the "put up or shut up" rule. If you oppose a living wage, live on what you are paying, with a journalist to keep you honest, for a month. Feel free to have someone from the National Chamber of Commerce keep you company. Wages will have to be readjusted every so often. Raising the minimum wage is part of addressing income inequality.

I want to raise middle-class income. Unions are one way. What are others? If wages had increased 25 cents a year since 1959, that would total $16.60. Put that quarter in a CD every year and raise wages $1.00 every four years. My $2.12 in 1959 was a "living wage" with raises to come. I believe in a living wage.

FOOD AND DRUG SAFETY

We would keep protections in place and add many. If your water smells like Teflon, that is a bad sign. It will soon be a crime. There will be requirements for research on over-the-counter medications and herbs, etc.

HEALTH

I am reading Peter Singer's *The Life You Can Save*. We will do pain management and hospice. It is no longer acceptable to spend your grandchildren's future on your last six months. Dying inexpensively with dignity is expected. We believe that life is sacred, and you have a right to die. Death education will be universal from grade schools through college. At least 133 million of us have chronic illnesses. We will have organ donation the default option. One is free to sign a statement that he or she doesn't want organ donation. Some Jews oppose it. We will have assisted suicide. If you are opposed to it, don't do it. As with an abortion, don't get one unless you want it. No one can impose his or her religious position. I'll repeat this. The only wall I believe in should be between government and religion. Premium health insurance policies will always be an option.

Aside: Warren Buffet: "For every dollar of exports, the government would issue an import 'chit'. Importers could import only if they had enough chits. If importers wanted to import more than exporters succeeded in exporting, the price of chits would rise until demand equaled supply: a market mechanism for restoring trade balance and helping restore the US economy to full employment." Do it.

China, we welcome the time when you become a democracy. We'll work with WTO countries. We have experts.

IRS

We will simplify our tax code and increase our enforcement. A relative worked there. Whoever thought identity theft would be a problem? We want more reviewers, better systems, and prosecution of tax criminals. Our system will need major reprogramming to support our new taxes. We'll aggressively pursue all the crooks. We'll build and pay more for some reviewers.

BORDER PATROL AND IMMIGRATION

You are welcome to 95 percent of them. We have other funding priorities. They are welcome to attend our retraining for other jobs.

HOMELAND SECURITY

We have spent a trillion dollars. Do you feel that much safer?

SOCIAL SECURITY

The US will deplete benefits by 2030. Then it will pay out 79 percent of scheduled benefits. In 2090, it will pay out 75 percent of scheduled benefits. We divide the money in the Social Security fund proportionally and manage our own Social Security. Preserve America retirees are going to have to live on less just like Reds will. AARP has 12 proposals. Every additional year increases benefits 6-8 percent; begin longevity indexing; recalculate the COLA; increase or eliminate the payroll tax cap; reduce benefits for higher earners; increase the payroll tax rate; tax all salary reduction plans; cover all newly hired state and local government workers; benefit improvements; increase number of years used to calculate initial benefits; and begin means testing Social Security benefits. I am vigilant about a new health plan. I know no other way to reduce seniors' costs.

ENTITLEMENTS

Everyone has to aggressively manage entitlements. Medicare, Social Security, and Medicaid are 53 percent GNP. Right now 81 million people are on Medicaid at an average cost of $5,800.

NATIONAL DEBT

9/11 cost $5.6 trillion. The war with Iraq cost over $3 trillion. Al Gore would never have invaded without proof of WMD (Weapons of Mass Destruction).

Aside: Expel college students who will not let others speak. That's outrageous. Put your energy into this. You are as totalitarian as the speakers you protest. My Penn State ethics students were stunned to learn that totalitarian countries killed poets. How can any country be so oppressive and freedom of speech so rare? Al Capp wrote Lil' Abner. Capp featured S.W.I.N.E.—Students Wildly Indignant about Nearly Everything. Leave SWINE behind. I learned this ditty from a Colorado forest ranger: Cy and I went to the circus. Cy got hit with a bowling pin. We got even with that mean ole circus. We both had tickets, but we wouldn't go in. Get even with that mean old conservative. Buy his book. Hold it up in silent protest of its contents and be a proud American that he or she can write it. A Providence Journal writer mentioned a book everyone should read. It was essays by a columnist that were so outrageously sexist, racist, and nihilistic. He might well be insane. First I was furious. Then, I thought, what a testimony to freedom of speech and press.

MILITARY

We shall have our own military and soldiers. Military experts think we shall always need an intervention or deterrent force. We agree. The money we spend is absurd. I saved a full-page article in the *New York Times* on March 27, 2017. Your paper should publish it. It was educational. All of Obama's money to cover crises cost the same as two new fighter jets. Two outdated fighter jets used to be able to outduel any one modern, advanced jet. Blues believe in nuclear disarmament. We should decrease the sheer chance of a nuclear accident. Diplomacy, foreign aid, and goodwill go a long way toward preventing wars. The better your diplomacy, the less weaponry you need. Soldiers should be paid more.

Aside: Microbes are scarier than countries. *Time* just did Pandemics.

VETERANS AFFAIRS

We spend more on ours.

UNITED NATIONS

We want to fund and staff it.

NATO

We would continue to participate. We see ourselves as world citizens. Each country will be expected to pay the goal of 2 percent of its GNP.

CAPITALISM

We still believe in it. I am reading Robert Reich's *Saving Capitalism: For the Many, Not the Few*. Every bank and other financial institutions will be regulated to free money for jobs and ideas. If a national bank can't do what we want, it will have to split. We want entrepreneurs. We agree that the cost to small businesses of federal, state, and local regulations is ridiculous. Banks have quit being banks. We will bring in our best economists and other experts to design ours.

Google, Facebook, Microsoft, Facebook, and Amazon are essentially monopolies. We oppose monopolies. Your monthly cable bill could be $28 except for Comcast and its world of cronies. Read and rage. EURO nations have blazing fast networks. We don't. That ends. We believe that competition improves quality and lowers cost, especially foreign competition. We will build and sell a 5G network.

ETHICS

We shall study these things together. Peter Singer wrote *Rethinking Life and Death, the Collapse of Our Traditional Ethics*. I have always thought and acted on his five. First, recognize that the value of a life varies. Second, take responsibility for your decisions. Third, respect a person's decisions to live or die. Fourth, bring children into the world only if they are wanted. Fifth, do not discriminate on the basis of species. I believe that the government should make euthanasia decisions, not physicians. They should be discussed and made law.

GERRYMANDERING

Preserve America will end gerrymandering. I did not know Rhode Island was doing it until I read a letter by someone from Common Cause. Everyone has to run as an independent. You run on issues, not party names. I've always thought that government should ideally reflect the population. That means 50 percent women and the proportion of minorities and general professions and workers. My family has engineers, nurses, firefighters, police, Physical therapy assistants, cooks, bartenders, and human resources staff. Single mothers should be nominated and elected.

ETHICS AND CONFLICT OF INTEREST

There will be no more working in government and then going to work someplace where you could influence funding. Revolving door ends. Ethicists will develop our policies; e.g., Citizens for Responsibility and Ethics and others. I taught ethics at Penn State. Ethicists will teach all of us. Corporations and contractors, it's a new day.

Things that should be ethical will now be enforced by law.

PRESERVE AMERICA QUALIFICATIONS

No one can run for any office that can't pass an exam on our new Preserve America Constitution, civics, ethics, geography, western civilization and US history. President Trump will be the last president to swear to uphold a Constitution he never read. We welcome Jews, Muslims, Hindus, atheists, and anyone else to be a **Preserve America** politician.

I lived in Texas, Tennessee, Kansas City, Maryland, Pennsylvania, California, Maine, and Rhode Island. I liked it everywhere. California is a place I lived, and I share more values with their state government. I am delighted that I live so close to New York City and Massachusetts. New York City welcomed most of the immigrants. Massachusetts fought in every war from the Revolution on. I like all of New England. I weep over my memory of how Texas used to be and Austin still is.

Washington, D.C. and White House, New York through Virginia, all will be **Preserve America**. Illinois, Pennsylvania, and Colorado will be **Preserve America**. All the West Coast will be **Preserve America**. Hopefully many other states will be too, will really move. My first recommendation would be Texas. Friends and family love it there. You get more football than you can watch. "God Bless Texas" is on my playlist. Martin Luther King, Jr. will be our new airport name.

We want to fund the Center for Disease Control (CDC) and National Science Foundation (NSF). Cancer and other diseases do not respect state lines. We shall fund the Smithsonian, parks, weather, and other government services.

Conservation and Public Parks

Someone called our national parks America's greatest idea. We shall gladly help pay our share for those that remain Republican. We oppose selling or polluting water.

Preserve America Summary

We are going to have our own president, House of Representatives, Senate, and judges. We want to be inclusive of all those who might wish to be. We want our Dreamers and Salvadorans to be citizens. It is the ethical and American thing to do.

Preserve America will have two presidents, one woman and one man. No vice president is needed. It is time to rethink what our presidential duties should be.

Senators

California gets six senators: two from Los Angeles, two from Sacramento to greater Los Angeles, two for the rest of the state. New York gets four senators: two from the greater New York City area and two from the rest of the state. Illinois gets four senators: two from greater Chicago and two from the rest of the state. Pennsylvania gets four senators: two each from greater Philadelphia and Pittsburg. Washington, DC gets two senators and at least three representatives. Massachusetts gets two. Connecticut gets two. New England (Maine, Vermont, New Hampshire, Rhode Island) shares two senators out of fairness. Preserve America will have two senators from each state, one woman and one man. There will be eight at large Black senators, four women and four men. There will be eight at large Latino senators, four women and four men. California will probably have at least one pair of Latinos, too.

Term limits

There should be term limits for everyone. Our president's should be the eight years we have now. Senators and representatives should have term limits. Our Supreme Court justices should have term limits. I leave it to others to decide.

GERRYMANDERING

I don't know who started it. It ends in **Preserve America** states. If we can't figure out how to do it fairly, a computer program will create our political districts. I read that if it were not for gerrymandering, Blues would control the House and Senate. Democrats won 1.4 times more votes in 2012. Wisconsin is slightly less than half Republican. They have some 60 of 99 seats. Pennsylvania has 800,000 more registered Democrat voters. Republicans have a 13 to 5 congressional advantage. That's so wrong.

Without Jefferson's many talents, I declare Preserve America's independence.

Preserve America opposes robocalls. It is now a crime. We'll locate you and sentence you to work in a national park for whatever vacation you would already have. Okay, maybe I just got one. Robocallers, this is your first warning.

We will have the "Martha Stewart" rule. Any white-collar crime greater than hers will be prosecuted. If convicted, he or she will be sentenced to no less than Martha Stewart was. There will be no more too rich to convict or too big to jail.

Wells Fargo executives of the future will be prosecuted under our new laws. Every future banker who contributed to the 2008 crash out of greed will serve time in our new Preserve America system. There will be no uncertainty that this is a crime.

BIG MERGERS

Blues are basically opposed to them. We want as many employees as possible. We want CEO pay advertised and golden parachutes discouraged. Let's see. You just violated law, stole hundreds of millions, and want hundreds of millions for your trouble. No. We shall discuss how bank executives are paid.

Net neutrality stays.

EVOLUTION

We believe in evolution. My third grade teacher, Ms. Castle, went over evolution using pictures from *Life* magazine. I got it at nine. Creationism is claptrap.

SCIENCE

We are all big on research. Everyone is required to read Bill Bryson's *A Short History of Nearly Everything*.

PUBLIC UNIONS

Can we capitate fire, police, teachers and attorneys? It is a new day. You are expected to self-monitor. There will be no more early retirement. There is no way the public can afford to pay for it. It was folly for anyone who understands statistics, trends, and public finance to have ever thought that was true. If you are tired of your job, quit. Do something else until Social Security kicks in. There are no more public bailouts. I am willing to have my taxes increase just as much as inflation, no more. We will have our own actuaries do public and private retirement funds. Unfunded pensions are a national disgrace. I lost a patient who thought he was going to get 14 percent on his funds. Irritated, he left. Democrats have let some unions get by with murder. We are pro union and pro accountability. The public is no longer on the hook. Early retirement is bankrupting states and cities. It ends. Do you feel so strongly that you would gladly give that person your own salary? Why should a state budget ever exceed cost of living? It shouldn't. One of the first *Providence Journal* articles was about a guy who was claiming as many years toward retirement as he was old and contesting it!

PROCESS

We will have local meetings to discuss how we want to develop our candidates and elect our president. The Electoral College ends. The person wins that gets the most votes. I consider it bad manners not to be a gracious loser. All discussions will begin with what I learned in high school debate: "My worthy opponent."

I think our current election process lasts too long and is unfair to states that have later voting versus earlier voting. Six months from start to finish should do it. People have thought about what campaigning for office and the rest of the process should be. They will educate the rest of us. Would a parliamentary form of government be better? We'll discuss the pros and cons. If you think you can't be deprogrammed from billions of dollars of lobbyist exposure, resign.

ECONOMICS

Here is a law. There are only two ways to grow economically: more population or more productivity. We are stagnant.

MANDATORY NATIONAL SERVICE

At Penn State, we did a study of what a mandatory national service would look like. Everyone has to go into the military or work for two years in public service, even the disabled, or some sort of Work Progress Administration (WPA) doing infrastructure and maintenance. As you will be able to tell from my attached essay on education, one problem is that too many resources are now going for special education. A service corps would allow one-on-one education for every child that needs it and free teachers. They could provide general childcare and elder care. I know people paying $10,000 and others paying $30,000 or more for childcare. I came away convinced that national service would be wonderful for the country if the dollars work. It could also be a time of developing work skills and socialization. I am 76 and would never want to live on my own without my sweetie. I repeat: elder care is needed.

I would have basic education offered very much like a community college and cosponsored by employers. It would create a standing, prepared military. We need character, accountability, and responsibility and smarter workers. I volunteer James Stavridis to lead a planning committee proportional. I am scared of white supremacists marching with rifles. I want a defense if they attack. A National Guard design or some other would be best. There will be as many women as men working on every **Preserve America** initiative. If you see six men standing together, it had better be the restroom. I think we can do all sorts of educational and service functions. Others will work on what our service could do. They will be an instant resource in times of disaster.

If enough men and women do not volunteer to be active, I propose another lottery.

I had a stay-at-home mom. She was perfect in that role. We value men and women as much as anyone else. We can volunteer to help disasters in Red states. Coastal Red states have to self-insure. We won't cover the costs of their own economic nonsense. We will have men and women ready. We will each have our own FEMA. Ours becomes rational.

GENDER

Preserve America should elect two presidents: a woman and a man. We don't need a vice president. Every pair of senators will be a woman and a man. If the men in my family were as competent as the women, we would be something. Puerto Rico can vote. I recommend Dee Dee Myers's *Why Women Should Rule the World*. I think there should be a cabinet or undersecretary position just for women. We reopen the Office for Domestic Violence. She is responsible: HEW goes to HEWW. Here is an edited piece about women by Alia Dastagir and a summary by the McKinsey Global institute on how women can help build our economy. Sexual harassment is common everywhere there are males. EEOC said the ratio of harassment is from 25 percent to 85 percent. The number of cases never reported was 75 percent.

I volunteer Dee Dee Myers and Sally Yates to think about governance and laws. They can lead a discussion and recruit representative women.

The following will be provided:

1. Access to birth control, prenatal, maternity care, maternity leave, mammograms, and breastfeeding supplies.

2. Sexual and domestic violence: One in three women have been a victim of some form of physical violence by an intimate partner, one in six American women will be the victim of an attempted or completed rape. We will uphold Title IX's federal guidance instructing colleges to combat campus sexual assault, and the Violence Against Women Act.

3. Paid family leave and childcare: We want paid family and medical leave, which allows people time off to care for a newborn, help a sick family member, or recover from a serious illness. We will provide up to 12 weeks of *unpaid* leave.

4. Our goal is three weeks of paid maternity leave to birth mothers and fathers. We want universal pre-K. "When you raise a law-abiding studious child, you are producing economic value," Ann Crittenden, author of *The Price of Motherhood*, said in urging taxpayers to do it.

5. Abortion is covered elsewhere. Planned Parenthood says an in-clinic abortion can cost up to $1,500 in the first trimester. We shall pay it. IUDs should be covered.

6. Equal pay for equal work: Our goal is to narrow and then eliminate the gap. "The majority of the current earnings gap comes from within occupation differences in earnings, rather than from between occupation differences," Claudia Goldin, a Harvard University labor economist, wrote in a 2014 paper.

The Pew Research Center said women make up nearly half the workforce, and are breadwinners in 40 percent of households with children, yet they are more likely than men to make compromises when the needs of children and family members collide with work, which they say negatively impacts their careers. Iceland is the most advanced country on equal pay. Claudia Goldin leads ways to increase a woman's income.

Again, my mom was wonderful. Dad told me never to let my wife work. Some women can't. Others don't want to. All of us appreciate any personal choice. Black women and Hispanic women financially make less.

A new **McKinsey Global Institute** report finds that $12 trillion could be added to global GDP by 2025 by advancing women's equality. The public, private, and social sectors will need to act to close gender gaps in work and society. Gender inequality is not only a pressing moral and social issue but also a critical economic challenge. If women—who account for half the world's working-age population—do not achieve their full economic potential, the global economy will suffer. While all types of inequality have economic consequences, in our new McKinsey Global Institute (MGI) report, *How advancing women's equality can add $12 trillion to global growth*, we focus on the economic implications of lack of parity between men and women. North America would have an incremental increase by 2025 of $3.1 trillion. **The US economy would be a fifth larger in 10 years.** Half of all federal positions will be women paid the same as men.

If I mention your name here in any context, I want you to work on Preserve America. If you wish I had mentioned your name, volunteer immediately to work on the policies after Preserve America is passed by Congress. I read that the Supreme Court has become too powerful. All of you are volunteered to work on what ours should be.

PERSONAL STATEMENT

I am well educated. I did a math proof in high school that got me scholarships. Oveta Culp Hobby—secretary of Health, Education, and Welfare—chose me as one of 15 high school graduates in the nation to receive a full Conoco scholarship and told me I could go to any college, just let them know about my award. The college would receive the same amount. Rice called my principal to let me know they would offer a full fellowship. I wanted to go to a Baptist college. I graduated first in my college, was nominated for a Danforth, was full-time faculty at Johns Hopkins in psychiatry, recognized for my teaching at Penn State, etc. Mary Ann Stewart, the most talented friend in my life, was an activist. She died in a Kansas City plane crash in 1963. Her death infuriated and motivated me. I did social justice, civil rights, equal rights, education, justice, hunger, marijuana/pain, a living wage, ecology, climate change, health reform, and others. I was born in poverty just like all my friends and family. My clothes fit in two small drawers and on one nail.

WALL STREET

Read Nathaniel B. Davis, "If War Can Have Ethics, Wall Street Can, Too". Page 211-215 in *Modern Ethics in 77 Arguments* by Peter Catapano and Simon Critchley. Also in the *New York Times*, 2017.

The National Anthem is optional. "This Land is Your Land" is easier to sing. Woody Guthrie was the most famous person to die of Huntington's.

I happen to think this country is in pretty good shape.

Aside: **92** percent of Americans born in 1940 made more than their parents. For 1950, it was **73** percent; for 1960, **62** percent; for 1970, **61** percent; for 1980, **50** percent. No wonder so many people are discouraged. Born in poverty in 1941, my American Dream was guaranteed. I teased my ethics class that their biggest mistake was their choice of parents. A second error was the year you were born. A third oversight was not being born rich like Trump.

TELECOM

I have friends in Hong Kong. It takes them seven seconds to download a high definition movie. The same is true in Seoul, Tokyo, Zurich, Bucharest, and Paris. Some pay as little as $30 a month. In Los Angeles, New York City, and Washington they can pay up to $300 a month and it takes 1.4 minutes for the fastest. My friends have a fiber-optic network. I want to pay $30 for seven seconds. Susan Crawford is a visiting professor at Harvard Law School. She wrote *Captive Audience: Telecom Monopolies in the New Gilded Age.* "The big internet providers have little reason to upgrade their entire networks because there has been so little pressure from competitors or regulators to do so." I volunteer Susan Crawford to be one new regulator. I can't find my list of other experts. Volunteer. Republicans and Democrats share the view that competition is the American way. I would prefer local competition and I owned more foreign cars than American. **Preserve America** will see what it takes.

IN SUMMARY

I read about a small business whose federal and state rules and regulations cost him $11,500 per employee. That's obscene. Our laws and regulations need change. We will fund at least $300 billion in school infrastructure. That includes heating, cooling, and other things.

General Motors had 600,000 workers in its glory. Apple, about the same size, has 70,000.

WOMEN

Dad was a Mason. We joined the First Baptist Church and went to the front to greet everyone. Dad said that three men were Masons. How could Mom tell? Masons had a secret handshake. That explains a lot about Republican males. The first part of the shake is necessary but not sufficient. Do you deny all science? Yes. Do you think that Republican males' right to control every woman's body was divinely inspired? Of course. Will you do everything in your power to deny women contraception and abortion all over the world? Yes. Welcome to our lodge.

I am old. We need young leaders with fresh ideas to act with energy and engagement. I defer to those who know more than me.

We need to move to a clean energy nation as California is doing. I'll ask someone else to write about the things California is already doing.

All of us will think about issues, write articles, and read together. We'll have to meet, discuss, and learn. Someone will need to file something official to get it on the state election calendars. We have much work until November 8.

"Give me your tired, your poor, your huddled masses yearning to breathe free, the wretched refuse of your teeming shore."

I was a clinical/social/community psychologist with 90 credits. We are choosing community development over chaos.

Nine of 10 rural areas now have citizens who appear foreign. Like everyone else, I think people will adapt. Diversity is difficult in the short run. I'll never get used to "press one for English." My daughter does not care. That will be the only thing my grandchildren ever knew. People will answer our phones.

Our new plan will lower health insurance. All of us have to live within our means. Some will suffer more than others. Every policy has side effects.

We will revise Dodd-Frank. We will have a fiduciary rule. I think it is dishonest not to have the standard of doing everything in your client's best interest. My sister and I inherited the same amount of money. I kept my Conoco stock. She invested with a local broker, but no fiduciary rule. I had $10,000 more in a few years. I know schoolteachers who would have fared better if their financial adviser had followed the fiduciary standard.

Repeat: Mandated service corps would allow one-on-one education for every child that needs it and provide childcare. I came away convinced that national service would be wonderful for the country. It could also be a time of developing work skills and socialization. I would have basic education offered very much like a community college and cosponsored by employers. It would create a standing, prepared military. I can't even guess the federal cost. Someone else will.

We shall fund public radio, arts, and legal services.

Brzezinski and Wasserman: We need clarity of thought and leadership, global stability. We need to project optimism and progress. Okay, Preserve America will.

I am listing my biggest issues:

- Preserving American democracy here and supporting it abroad.
- Climate change.
- Tax reform.
- Decreasing income inequality.
- Our new government health plan.
- Education from pre-K through college.

Our new Constitution that will spell out several protections including the ERA. Half of every committee will be women. Half of all federal offices will be held by women. Women will be paid the same for the same work. We shall support homemakers. We encourage families and parents. Childcare will be covered.

Infrastructure will cost us $1.5 trillion more or less.

I repeat: we have about $10 trillion in unpaid taxes.

JUSTICE AND PRISONS

Preserve America states are no longer world outliers. We are seen as dealing with crime in a humane way. We redefine felonies. All drug users are released.

Mandatory alternative service of two years at some time between ages 18 and 28. This is my only novelty. We shall educate everyone.

This will be used as parole and probation. It will provide training in skills needed in the workplace. It will be a source of jobs for seniors. Armed services are an option. They will work with the IEP (Individualized Education Program) children and free teachers to teach. They will staff parks. They will do small-scale infrastructure. They will do childcare. Military bases will be used for both military and general education/training. We will use it to build old-fashioned character.

HOUSING
We will enforce fair housing rigorously.

JOBS
We have a shortage of mechanics, truck drivers, electricians, plumbers, etc.

RULES AND REGULATIONS
Abolish them unless they are obviously dangerous and start all over. We want thoughtful ones.

TORTURE
I had a clinical psychology practice in California. A psychiatrist asked me to treat two female torture victims pro bono. I said, "Of course." Both women were from a dictatorship in South America. They had been raped many times and physically abused in such vivid ways I won't even tell, lest you can't sleep either.

Although we may never know with complete certainty the identity of the winner of this year's Presidential election, the identity of the loser is perfectly clear. It is the Nation's confidence in the judge as an impartial guardian of the rule of law.
— Justice John Paul Stevens [Dissent] Bush v. Gore (2000)

In a five to four vote, the Supreme Court chose George Bush who had fewer popular votes over Al Gore who had more.

"These are the times that try men's souls. The summer soldier and the sunshine patriot will shrink from their duty. He that stands now deserves the love and thanks of man and woman. Tyranny, like hell, is not easily conquered. Yet we have this consolation with us, the harder the conflict, the more glorious the triumph. It is dearness only that gives everything its proper value."

"...go from me cursed into everlasting fire. Prepared for the devil and his angels, for I was hungry and you did not feed."

We want a living wage. Pope Francis said it is a great sin not to take care of the poor.

Aside: I could not beat my cat, Gus, at Bogle. No, I won't remember your name. My grammar and spelling are gone. Enough of the statistical, analytical, modeling part remains. My daughter is 50. Here is my immodest forecast: Most of the states that do not vote Preserve America will vote that way in her lifetime or go bankrupt. Our Constitution and form of Truth, Justice, and the American way for everyone will win over your Rich White Male government.

LGBTQ

I was unlikely to have been gay. I would stare at the bras in a Sears catalog for hours. Mom never let one parenting moment go and said nothing. When I was a teenager, Dad said that some men would ask me for sex; I should be respectful, and say no. That some men prefer to have sex with other men was the single most astonishing thing Dad told me. If you are one of the men reading this who propositioned me, I hope I said no in a respectful way. Here is a memory of how many boys in California said they had had sex with another boy: 40 percent.

The fact that other Christians don't love LGBTQs out of the goodness of their heart is flat-out wrong. I recommend Daniel A. Helminiak's, *What the Bible Really Says About Homosexuality*. For those who still don't care, I have only this last Christian observation to share: I believe in an all-loving God. You believe in a God who makes exceptions for LGBTQs. I am putting LGBTQs, abortion, and women's rights into my Constitution to affirm and protect them.

When Mom would take me to Wichita Falls to window shop, the 5/10 cents store had colored and white water fountains. Colored people always sat across from us, never next to us. There were white and colored bathrooms. Just, when I think about that type of ignorance and prejudice...

Sodomy was against the law in 42 states.

Your version: The moment David and Jonathan made love to each other, David became so evil in your mind that neither you nor your supporters would bake a cake for David and Jonathan's wedding. David would go to his American death hearing nothing but cries of "unclean" just as lepers once did. I am way too late to save Jews from Nazis. Hitler would have been happy to deport Jews just like you would be happy to deport the LGBTQ community. Six million plus men, women, and children, all Jews, were killed. When the Muslim killed the gay/lesbian club goers in Orlando, Florida, one Baptist preacher somewhere said if he could he would happily mow them all down with a machine gun. Hitler thought Jews were impure and hated them. You must somehow think the same about the LGBTQ community.

Mike was a grandfather. His father was a marine in WWII. He was a marine in Vietnam. When his first grandchild was born, to my delight and surprise, Mike volunteered several hours a day for two days a week to care for him. When his second grandson was born one year later he did the same. No grandfather was more diligent. He hovered like a hawk. "Carl, I am never going to have anything happen to them on my watch." It is now my turn to say, no, I am not going to have anything in my government happen to any of my grandchildren on my watch.

CHINA

In our Republican leaders' eagerness to give each other phony tax cuts and in their new isolationism, I think they took their eye off of you, Xi Jinping. The minute that Xi Jinping dies China will vote to become a democracy.

More than everything else combined, Japan went from an imperialist country to a wonderful trading country. I fear you want go from a trading partner to imperialist. I made two business trips to China and think you no more represent your average citizen than Mao. Preserve America will promote democracy. I have been to Shanghai and Hong Kong and have friends and acquaintances there. **Preserve America**, a democracy, will go back to being the world leader.

When Walter Cronkite was liberal and conservatives watched Huntley Brinkley, this bizarre spin on truth would never have happened. I am 76. In the words of Will Campbell: Having nothing better to do, why not save America? I remember before it was bought off by special interests; I have no idea how many trillions of dollars it has been. The Consumer Protection Agency (CPA) has recovered $20 billion so far. Banker in yesterday's *New York Times*: Like most Republicans, I oppose the CPA. Entitlements work both ways. He is opposed to a poor person getting in the first place, and openly says bankers and other special interests are entitled to billions.

FRIVOLOUS LAWSUITS

I think that Rhode Island could lead the nation in what I would call frivolous lawsuits and awards so out of perspective to the rest of us.

One of my Baptist professors was an attorney. Tarrant County judges were so corrupt that it was a common joke to say that voters should just write in the name of a WWI vet who sold newspapers. One election year it happened. The guy won. His winning was challenged. There was no Texas law that said you had to be an attorney and he became a judge. He said, "I don't know what is legal. I have spent my whole life thinking about what is right and wrong. I'll make my decisions accordingly and tell you why." Lawyers preferred him to any other judge. A famous lawyer was called Bare Foot Wallace. Let's call our new screeners who act out of ethical and public responsibilities, Bare Foot Wallace. I have had three Rhode Island experiences in which I could have sued. In one I was on a Fiji cruise when I stepped on the second step going down, and it broke, leaving my back sore and painful. The cruising company offered me $300 off any future cruise.

The guy who collected some $7 million for loss of a leg would have made Bare Foot Wallace indignant. She would have said let's talk about something in the hundreds of thousands. I want our money to go to medications for the poor or elder care. She would have sent him off to read an ethics book. From 1969 to 1970, 24 of us belonged to a house church covenant community in Nashville. A mixture of Baptists and Methodists we usually tithed. Runaways were common. We decided to buy a house together for runaways who were hungry and living on the street. We had already bought the house when one of the runaways' parents' lawyers wrote to us. He said his clients would sue our socks off and ask for damages if we went ahead. They would prefer their kids to be either on the streets or home. I vowed to never to be one of those parents.

When I got my Johns Hopkins position, I wanted to live in Columbia, Maryland, the new town. Rouse's child planners had built my favorite playground of all time. Part of it was for adults. I took my daughter there. All but the swings, slides, and iron climbers had been closed. An attorney had said that if his child got injured there he would sue Columbia. Enough, let's talk about what type of person a Bare Foot Wallace can be. A "Bare Foot" person can be male or female, Black, Hispanic, and others.

FREE ASSOCIATION

Jews and Californians. When I went to Boys' State in Texas in 1959, one boy came down and said there is a Jew down the hall. I had read *Jew and Children of Israel* hundreds of times. Jew sounded exotic and foreign. It had not occurred to me that they lived in Texas. So down we go to his room. The ringleader says, "He looks just like us."

"Our president gets imaginary calls from imaginary friends. Wake me when it's over." Wake that woman up. We need her.

My Bowie, Texas history teacher, Mrs. Henry, talked about the Civil War. She said that the Ku Klux Klan marched when she was a child. One pair of shoes was distinctive. It belonged to a deacon in her church. I had never heard of the KKK, so I went home and asked Mom. She said they approved of Negros being lynched and mutilated, were evil, and going to hell. It made no difference what these men did in church. I told my daughter KKK, white supremacists, and Nazis are evil and going to hell. My grandkids know little about the KKK. When they do it won't be in **Preserve America**. I promised myself that I would be vigilant and act against evil, never dreaming that my president would embolden them to march in Virginia. Before Trump, I knew very few people who hated other people. I know tens of millions. A Charlottesville paper follows:

> "White nationalists and supremacists Unite the Right rally had a Friday night surprise. They were going to march in a torchlight procession — a symbolic gathering meant to evoke similar marches of Hitler Youth and other ultra-right nationalists

> "...a horrific 24 hours in this usually quiet college town that would come to be seen by the nation and world as a day of racial rage, hate, violence and death.

> "At 9:30 a.m., about 30 clergy members clasped arms and began

singing 'This Little Light of Mine.' Twenty feet away, the white nationalists roared back, 'Our blood, our soil!'"

Trump said they are good people, supported the marchers, and criticized the protestors. I repeat, no, there isn't some good in a KKK, white supremacist, or Nazi. They are spiritually evil and going to hell. You don't condone evil like the alternate-right, much less openly support it like Steve Bannon. There was a civil war over slavery. The south lost. Many died. We fought against Nazis. Millions died, from 6 million Jews to 2 million others. Nazis and Japanese killed soldiers and civilians with almost equal abandon. I never dreamed Nazis, KKK, and white supremacists would march in my lifetime and have a president ambivalent at best about what I think is evil, much less support it. I will not live with a government that does not see evil as clearly as I do. It is hard enough for my kids. Thankfully, DC and Maryland, where my grandchildren live, are Blue states. The vote will not be even close. Dietrich Bonhoeffer died trying to assassinate Hitler. "We must learn to regard people less in the light of what they do or omit to do, and more in the light of what they suffer."

Preserve America will now be able to support our many allies: Germany, England, France, Australia, and all other democracies. China happily fills the world leadership gap every four years. Democrats want EPA in place. Republicans don't. We want regulations in place to protect the average citizen. Republicans are dismissing and reducing claims against predators even as I write. Democrats think a strong state department promotes democracy and prevents wars. Republicans think the smaller the better. You can never replace the leaders who are being fired/laid off even now. Every four years, white supremacists and Nazis march boldly with a government that condones them. Every four years we have a government that is outraged by both. Steve Bannon publicly supports white supremacists, KKK, and Nazis. Our new laws will make harassing phone calls and threatening emails unlawful. Just when I thought Trump's deporting people had no practical use, along come Nazis. Say anything you want to each other. Make one threat and we vote to deport you to some country that also hates Jews. We find out whatever that country's slur word is for gays. Your t-shirts will say on one side that you are not one and on the other side that you are. If they throw you off a rooftop in their hatred and confusion, well, there you go.

LGBTQ

When the gay bar residents were gunned down, one Baptist preacher said he would happily machine-gun everyone gay. I'll do my best to protect you.

Nazis

Bernie Liberman and I have been friends since Johns Hopkins. What was Sophie's choice in William Styron's novel? She had two children. The Nazis told her that unless she chose one to live, they would kill them both. Joel Elkes was chairman of psychiatry at Hopkins. What was his father's choice? He and another committee could choose which Jews lived longer before the gas chambers. The person who does our mandatory Holocaust/genocide component will tell you more. Howard Gardner has the curriculum I like best. He chose the Holocaust as his example of good versus evil. I think "the only good Indian is a dead Indian" with even more millions killed was the greatest racial atrocity outside of Russia and China. United States slavery is third.

I have a Black grandson and most of my friends are Jews. There was no enemy whom I would have more happily killed than Nazis. WWII Japanese and Nazis killed civilians by the hundreds of thousands. Germany and Japan are now friends. Make one threat and off you go until we can decide what to do with you. Even "Nazi lives matter" would irritate me. Say anything to each other. Carry all the signs you want. No more threats, or off you go until we can talk about our laws.

Preserve America will have its own Constitution, senators, representatives, and judges. Someone wrote a book called *The Impossible Presidency*. Others have thought about the same problem. We want an optimal presidency for our two new presidents that will last as long as possible, not be impossible. What role should our own Supreme Court play in preserving the separation of powers and their roles? I worry about injustice for those not traditionally represented. We'll have legal aid.

I am worried mentally and physically for my children. I want a domestic army for lots of reasons. I want to be able to defend against massive armed gangs. I repeat: most of my friends are Jews. I cannot imagine what they think about rising anti-Semitism here. I have had a dozen or so Black friends or colleagues. I have a Black grandson. I know lots of gays and lesbians.

I am not a Black. I am not a Jew. I cannot believe this is happening in America. White supremacists terrify me. Muslims don't. The GOP exults in their wickedness. No, I am not going to leave a $1.5 trillion tax cut/federal debt for my children and grandchildren to pay off. The two greatest problems in America are discrimination and income inequality. The tax cut to the rich makes it worse. Blacks have $5 of wealth for every $100 of white wealth. If not for discrimination, those numbers would be close. Lyndon Johnson and I believe in Medicare, Medicaid, and a strong government that does things for the average person that no state can. We know how to stop business predators and lower health costs. We can make taxes so simple that our government does them and sends them for us to sign and goes after abusers. We think white crime is serious.

Preserve America will be fair, a government that takes care of the middle class I am now part of and the poor I was born into. It is outrageous not to believe in a living wage. "Living" should give it away. The tax bill was wicked from the start. There will never be any outcome that is not wicked. I am not the least bit confused that white supremacists are evil. I don't want a government the least bit confused about it, either. "Blood and soil" is pure evil. Not denouncing "blood and soil" is its own evil.

> *Rising tensions between the U.S. and North Korea have an unsettling chance of escalating, MIT security experts said at a public forum on Tuesday — but are also manageable given the right approach by U.S. leaders. "I think you can get inadvertent war," said Jim Walsh, a senior research associate in MIT's Security Studies Program (SSP) and a nuclear security expert who has visited North Korea in the past. "It's still an unlikely event," "I would remind you that improbable events do happen. ... I am more worried than I have been before."*

> *"I think China believes that the North Koreans are developing nuclear weapons for perfectly [logical] reasons," said Taylor Fravel, an associate professor of political science at MIT and interim director of MIT's Center for International Studies (CIS). Fravel, a leading expert on China's foreign-policy conflicts, added that Chinese leaders, who maintain their own nuclear arsenal, likely view North Korea's weapons as "an insurance policy, one they [China] can see in their own history."*

> —MIT

It is not Rex Tillerson's fault and it is not Trump's fault either that he can't tell right from wrong, is paranoid and delusional. Trump is too mentally unstable to own a gun. Tell me he would not have shot that California illegal immigrant. No, he cannot attack North Korea. No US warmonger can attack either. Preserve America will have the diplomats negotiate with Kim Jong-un and experts educate Rex Tillerson. We will have a strong international commitment to democracy. It is ours to do. It is sheer madness to want millions of noncombatants and hundreds of thousands of combatants to die in a conventional war rather than accept North Korea as a nuclear power.

I volunteer Joe Biden, Susan Rice, and Madelyn Albright to negotiate a peaceful settlement on behalf of Preserve America. Jim Walsh and Vipin Narang are experts that Rex Tillerson does not have. Rex Tillerson can use them or not. He can be part of it or send other representatives. I am letting all Republican politicians and our generals know Preserve America will negotiate a peaceful settlement. Your job is to keep Trump from attacking North Korea and out of it.

To: Mr. Kim Jong-un, North Korea

You will never back down. We are sending a Preserve America negotiating team. I apologize for President Trump's outrageous behavior. His scare tactics scare all of us. Your threats scare me. No it is not right to declare you evil because you are a Communist and go to war. Maybe six people in America feel that way. The moment Trump hears this on Fox News, we are taking him out of it and locking him up if necessary. Even if we had no choice, we could live with your being another nuclear party. I read that millions died when your crops failed. No one wanted more of your women, children, and men to starve. Here is Preserve America's deal of carrot and stick. Carrot: We accept you as a nuclear power. We bring our US troops in South Korea home. We bring home our battleships. We bring home our fighter jets and military planes. We lift the embargo. We lift sanctions. You stop your hackers. We negotiate other things such as no more missile testing and no more threats by either of us. Now the stick: I agree with Trump. If you attack South Korea or another ally without nuclear weapons, we will use nuclear weapons in defense. No, we will not nuke you first. I'd be shocked if even 50,000 of your citizens would prefer to be dead Communists versus live South Koreans. No more Americans, non-combatant North Koreans, or South Koreans are going to die.

An estimated 2 million noncombatants died in Vietnam. My Penn State friend, Rustom Roy, gave a talk in 1975: no graduating class of 2000. He was convinced that something accidental would launch a nuclear war. So am I. War may be inevitable with China, and I hope not. It would drive me nuts to go to war when China was right, not us. Men are evil, women not so much. If there is a way to do away with nukes, Preserve America would be part of it, however unlikely that seems now. We can certainly reduce our nuclear arsenals. I read while at Penn State that Russia had added State College as a direct target. Again, I apologize. Do not do or say anything until our diplomatic team arrives to go over terms.

In one year, it will be public what Preserve America is doing. They can keep all the secret meetings and donations. Our donations will be public. Our laws will have open, transparent meetings. We will have as broad a representation as possible. We have many men and women who are scholars. Experts will back into our mix, as well the American Bar Association for our courts.

Preserve America notes for my grandchildren: "It is now my turn to make sure nothing happens to you on my watch." We all have family and friends who are gays and lesbians. Nothing will happen to them, Jews, Blacks, or other minorities, on my watch. No, I won't leave you with $1.5 trillion in federal debt that I never approved. It is hard for me to believe and accept that these republicans have children of their own. Dad taught me to "hunt and whittle and give just a little." He said do what is right and never compromise on something I think wrong, much less evil.

I think transparency should be part of all our laws. Everything should be public until it is time to negotiate in private. I subscribed half of my life to the *New York Times* and half to the *Washington Post.* By luck, the *Providence Journal* turned out to be a good paper, not one a friend once called his local excuse. Be vigilant about all their concerns. Google Vascha's "The Real Coup Plot is Trump's" and Paul Krugman's "Facts"; both have a well-known liberal bias. I have hundreds of such clippings about things I want you to read when you are older to let all of you know what other people wanted and feared. No, a transgender child does not serve Satan.

Take care. It is time to stop a war with North Korea. Congress, please vote to pass **Preserve America** legislation.

Thank you,
Carl Young, PhD

DECEMBER 25, 2017

Is Donald Trump amoral?

I am going to explain why Mr. Donald Trump can't help himself and never will be able to. I have studied history, ethics, the brain, and psychological disorders. I am a retired clinical psychologist and taught amoral ethics in Penn State's required ethics course. Based on Trump's behavior, my diagnosis is that he was born amoral. Trump cannot be accountable. His Axis II personality disorders are not his fault. His statements suggest a "pervasive pattern of disregard for and violation of the rights of others; lack of empathy; bloated self-image; and manipulative and impulsive behavior." He is the most narcissistic politician ever. We now know he is paranoid, delusional, with sociopathic symptoms.

"Amoral: lacking a moral sense; unconcerned with the rightness or wrongness of something; unprincipled, without standards, without morals, without scruples, Machiavellian, unethical." Memorize.

"Personality disorders are a class of mental disorders characterized by enduring maladaptive patterns of behavior, cognition, and inner experience, exhibited across many contexts and deviating markedly from those accepted by the individual's culture. These patterns develop early and are inflexible." Study.

From 1.8 million years ago in the Serengeti Plain, it has been in the best interest of Homo sapiens to have a balance between selfishness and cooperation. Our brains have evolved with "moral" centers. Things that ethicists hold dear are a mystery to Trump. His brain has no right/wrong area. Nothing and no one can change him. That part of his brain that could respond to external feedback is missing.

In all fairness to the public at large, no one has a compass other than experience and schooling for thinking about amoral people. I am educated and a competent psychologist and diagnostician. Amoral people are hard to think about. They are even harder to deal with. Just when we think they have exceeded every possible social boundary, they do or say something even more excessive that dupes us again.

On my clinical psychology internship, I had my first experience with sociopaths, psychopaths, and other Axis II personality disorders. I was no match for them. A psychologist who thinks he or she can treat your typical Axis II patient is foolhardy.

A graduate student at Penn State studied juvenile male Axis II amoral offenders. He said, "These amoral juveniles were not 'human' as we use that term."

In ethics, I said: "The amoral person makes out like a bandit until he or she meets another amoral person who is just as willing and motivated to violate social rules."

Are Americans more or less intolerant than they were two years ago? Producing bigotry is the only thing Trump has been really good at. He is actually proud of it.

I inherited two ethics books: Willard Gaylin, Ira Glaser, Stephen Marcus, and David Rothman's *Doing Good: The Limits of Benevolence,* and Sissela Bok's *Lying.* Trump would find both titles perplexing. Why would people want to do good? Bok addresses why people should not lie. Trump does not even try to agree with himself. He makes statements that are specific, can be checked, and are wrong. No fact is safe with him. He has made some 12,000 or so lies or misstatements so far, with no end in sight.

Ethics was required of 4,000 undergraduates in the College of Human Development at Penn State. Dan Katkin asked me to compare moral, amoral, and immoral behavior in the criminal justice module and one graduate course in social policy.

Moral people have limits. No matter where you draw your line, Trump is willing to cross it. Every day someone tries to justify Trump's behavior. All of which is nonsense when you are up against an amoral person. It is so hard to keep this in mind. I can. Some can't. His past world was made up of suckers and losers. That view worked amazingly well for him. I don't know what Trump is going to say or do next. He doesn't either.

Sissela Bok said: "Only a moral pygmy would say, 'I am hiding a Jew in my attic.'" Only a moral pygmy would think Trump is ethical, fair, and/or principled.

The scariest book I have mostly read is Theodore Millon's *Disorders of Personality: DSM III: Axis II.* Millon goes into more detail about Trump and others like him. If you just read random pages, don't say I didn't warn you.

Questions

Could you even make 260 campaign promises? No problem for President Trump.

Could you even say "elect me because I am a good business manager" when you had filed four bankruptcies and bragged about making a financial killing? Piece of cake for amoral Trump.

Would it occur to you to brag about not paying taxes when you and I do? He did.

If you were a billionaire could you promise to give a measly million dollars to veterans when no veterans organization reported getting any? President Trump did and did not.

Call Mexicans rapists, and say you are going to build a wall and make Mexico pay for it? Even as I write, Trump wants that wall built with no moral idea that money would be better spent on infrastructure. He said it. It must be true.

Say "drain the swamp" and then hire billionaires, cronies, and your own family? Piece of cake, no problem, just another day at the office, who cares how I behave?

In summary, all of the rational appeals in the world will not affect Trump. The moral center in his brain was missing at birth. He is the classical amoral person. I repeat: many amoral people end up in prison. Trump was elected.

Trump won't stop. No one thought Trump was going to be a gracious loser. We now know he is the all-time worst winner. He continues to want Hillary Clinton locked up. Nearly all of us have brains with "moral" centers. We are socialized in a thousand ways that Donald Trump never could be; 99 percent of his right/wrong brain area is missing. All of the amoral prisoners we studied at Penn State were born that way. By the time they were teenagers, their amoral behavior was in full bloom. President Trump's thoughts and behaviors won't, maybe can't, change.

President Trump demonstrates modest intelligence. His brain tells him he's smarter than anyone else. "Only I can fix it." He does not know that 100 million of us were born smarter. Could you say, "I've never done anything I felt sorry about"? Alabama's voters might forgive him of his sins. Traditionally, one has to repent to be forgiven by God. How are Jesus and Trump alike? Jesus did not sin. Trump thinks he didn't either. I could give dozens of amoral examples. No church or charity reported getting one dollar from our most famous billionaire. He gives imaginary VA donations. He has imaginary calls from imaginary friends. His new press secretary said she would not call any of his lies really lies. "For the president, they are all true." I see no violation either. Google "Pathological Lying Disorder," "Esposito," or "sociopathic liar."

I am from Texas and have friends and family in Houston and Austin. Scenes from Harvey's damage were heartbreaking. President Trump said nothing about the deaths and comforting those who knew and loved them. I heard nothing about the homes and businesses that had been devastated—not one word of spontaneous empathy, as usual for someone amoral. Harvey reminded me that Trump had allegedly defrauded an insurance company after a storm.

Google: "Trump took $17 million in insurance for damage few remember." The title says it all. Read it.

The guy has always been shameless. The question is: can he help it? As an amoral billionaire, he could care less.

No one has a moral compass other than experience and study for thinking about or dealing with someone who has no conscience. His cabinet, senators, and Kelly know how impossible he is to deal with. He never thinks he's wrong and attacks and threatens friends and foes alike. He is still obsessed with Hillary Clinton. He still wants to lock her up for a crime she never committed.

260 campaign promises popped into Trump's mind. He kept his racist, sexist, and negating-anything-Obama promises. Family and friends got a ranch in Texas. He cancelled the Trans-Pacific Partnership. TPP brought us $1.5 billion in annual beef sales, plus international help with China and North Korea. Go figure.

In ethics: "the amoral person could care less about the truth or you. They violate social norms at will. They will tell you anything to get what they want." Trump is a born con.

Ask any amoral expert about Donald Trump. I could go on. So can they. So can you.

Take care,
Carl Young, Ph.D.

To: Austin American Statesman

Even more children will die. Google said 700,000 Americans searched for "abortion" in 2016. How can one be opposed to both abortion and contraception? That's immoral; forget Christian. Worldwide, 47,000 die from self-induced abortions. Five million women are injured. And 220 million women want to stop pregnancies.

Dirt poor, I got my first gun and a King James Bible for Christmas when I was nine. I had no idea that the bible would turn out to be more dangerous than any gun.

I think abortions should be legal and safe. Ideally women would use contraception so that abortions become rare. There is no reason to permit abortions after 20 weeks. There are cultural things as well as religious. I recognize its moral importance to many. I was reared believing in the separation of church and state.

Correspondent: "I think Democrats would rather lose than give up abortion." That's not even close. Your freedom of religion should never infringe on mine. Here is an early bumper sticker: If you oppose abortion, don't have one.

Why would you think you should be able to keep anyone who feels the way I do from having an abortion because of your religion? That's unconstitutional and immoral. You would think they would want to keep atheists from breeding.

Right after Trump was elected, a woman drove from Texas to a DC prolife rally to oppose my own family and friends in Texas being able to have one. I think she should have been locked up until she passed a test on our Constitution and read Peter Singer, an atheist. He wrote *Ethics in the Real World: 82 Brief Essays on Things That Matter*. He has more compassion for the poor suffering down-and-out than any of you. I expected you to be Christian models. Dad was a Baptist Universalist; so Peter Singer, President Trump, and you make his heaven. Mom thought there was a hell.

After passing Singer's ethical exam, they are told never to use prolife out of context again. Being opposed to your own abortion is okay. Being opposed to mine isn't. Saying you are prolife is outrageous and never left unchallenged.

Some native Texan should tell President Trump that if Santa Anna had not been so incompetent, Mexico might be building a wall on Red River to keep us out. For those of you not from Texas, our senior trip was originally 12 days. I wanted to add a day. We did and went to Canada: "13 days of glory at the siege of Alamo."

Pope Francis called Trump not a Christian. Catholic bishops called out Bannon.

Jerry Falwell's favorite president can't quote John 3:16. Franklin Graham and evangelicals are setting new records for Christian hypocrisy. In all of history, there has never been anyone whom President Trump would have more happily deported than Jesus. They have not said a thing. What is it about speaking out about and/or resigning over President Trump's values? Chinese have a strong preference for sons. Indians prefer sons to daughters, too. During my lifetime, 20 million or so females have been aborted or allowed to die as infants in China and India.

At least one religion opposes abortion. All Hindus do. "I am a Male Texas Republican Hindu. My religion opposes abortion. So do I." Hindus will instantly understand and accept your religious position. Don't mistreat women in the name of Jesus. President Strickland: "It is not a sin to be ignorant. It is a sin to stay that way." "Boys, pray for a pretty wife. It doesn't cost anymore."

I am 80. Permit me an Archer City story. I was 11. My sister, Pat, was 6. Dad said,

I am not saying there are not good reasons to oppose abortion. Hindus—how can you practice mass infanticide of females and oppose abortion?

Catholics and evangelicals, how can you say you are right-to-life and oppose contraception? Texas Republicans—how can you believe in the sanctity of life from conception to birth, and not so much afterwards? It is disgraceful and shameful that Texas women have some of the worst health outcomes in America. Fund Planned Parenthood. Unless you are Hindu, don't say you oppose abortion for religious reasons.

"God Bless Texas" is on my playlist. Don't make God regret it.

Carl Young, PhD.

EDUCATION AND SPECIAL EDUCATION
Providence Journal in 2012:

My turn: What we spend in public schools on special education (SE) "developing kids" I think is the major explanation why all the other kids became **1 to 2 percent** dumber/scored lower each year for **54** years and was additive. This is appalling and has to be rebalanced.

I have talked about it since 1967. I have never written. I shall tell my past role, provide two examples of the urgency, and give my solution.

I got my PhD in psychology from George Peabody College for Teachers (Vanderbilt) with a minor in special education. I worked out of the Nashville mayor's office and knew many leaders in public education. At Johns Hopkins, my chairman asked me to be the Hopkins representative at two public schools. For 15 years, I watched parents allege their child had "special needs" that could not be met in the regular classroom. The parent wanted and usually got more of the school budget reallocated to his or her child.

Parents who did not think their child had special needs seldom showed up. Why would they? When I did, sometimes I would concur with the parents about SE. Usually, I wouldn't agree. Three types of equality follow: resources, opportunity, and outcome. SE parents argued that their child deserved not the same opportunity but the same outcome. These parents wanted as many resources for their child as possible. No one got more money when this SE child was born with or developed this condition. Fixed school budgets were being reallocated from regular kids to "developing kids" with dire consequences. I said my best professional guess was this will likely make the other children score lower **1-2 percent** annually and be additive. The SE parent did not understand, did not believe me, or didn't care. The **1 to 2 percent** trend was evident to me as a psychologist trained in statistics and analytics. I understand budgets. I taught social policy.

No one can detect annual changes of **1 to 2 percent** until they are cumulative.

In 1983, *A Nation at Risk* was published. *A Nation at Risk* said public school students had been scoring lower for **20** years. I know small towns in Texas where kids still learn as much and score as high. I know of none in Rhode Island. *A Nation at Risk* should have eliminated any public/parental doubt. It didn't. I quit saying anything. American kids continued to learn less. This has been going on for **54** years.

No one wants life to be unfair. It is. Donnie, a cousin my age, was profoundly retarded. Uncle Fern died, leaving Aunt Ruth with two small daughters. I have a rare genetic disorder that killed my baby sister, just as it will me. All of us think our education system should cover some special needs. It now covers too many.

New York City spends less than **33** percent of its school budget educating normal kids. My Texas hometown spent over **90** percent. I thought **15** percent would make a difference. Anyone might think **30** percent would. Bowie spent almost **300 percent** more than New York City. I don't know Rhode Island's percentage. I went to a wedding last summer and met a new, New York City schoolteacher. Her full-time job is teaching six autistic spectrum kids.

Parents, teachers, and kids feel happy when students make A's and B's no matter how much the child is actually learning. Grade inflation in public schools and colleges has masked how little the students are learning. In 1960, tuition at the University of Texas was $54 a semester. My private college was $15 a semester hour. We graduated with little, if any, college debt. Never have college students paid so much and learned so little. The SAT scores became so low they were renormed. My grandsons will receive 100 bonus points that my daughter didn't. College student, what you are paying is inexcusable. There are proposals to force universities with endowments over $1 billion to contribute a fixed percentage to students in need. What you are learning is your responsibility. Study the two to three hours out of class for every hour in class that used to be the standard for an A or B. Here is an ad anyone my age finds ludicrous: "Best TVs for Dorm Rooms." Sure.

It is almost impossible for parents to know how well their kids are really doing. I lived in Maryland and taught at Hopkins. I have chosen a Blue Ribbon school there. "Blue Ribbon" means that its students score in the top 15 percent in Maryland. Wouldn't you be elated if your child brought home A's and B's from a Blue Ribbon school? I would. But wait. "Blue Ribbon" may mislead the parents. I am going to give two sets of statistics about this school's scores on PARCC and remediation.

Public education became so bad that states decided to let parents know how much children learned or didn't learn. Every Maryland and Rhode Island child is now tested. The tests were designed by educators and employers and titled Partnership for Assessment of Readiness for College and Career (PARCC). Employers have complained for decades about how little high school graduates know and how poor their work skills and habits were. Thirty percent of high school sophomores couldn't calculate a 15 percent tip.

I know as much about testing and its inherent problems as anyone.

Here are the PARCC scores for this Maryland Blue Ribbon School. There are two passing grades on PARCC: "meets expectations" and "exceeds expectations." Not one student on Algebra I (**ZERO**), out of the **2,680** tested, "exceeded expectations" on Algebra I. Results: **43** percent "met expectations" on Algebra I, **57** percent did not meet expectations. In grade 10, **2,030** students took English Language Arts and Literacy. Results: **15** percent "exceeded expectations," **35** percent "met expectations," **50** percent did not meet expectations.

PARCC scores in Rhode Island are similar to Maryland. I find them depressing and galling.

I have a second example of how bad public education has become. "Remediation" refers to college courses that high school graduates are required to take for no credit. A whopping **66** percent of the students at the Community College of Rhode Island take remedial courses. We are asking community colleges to educate students they were never designed to. I can afford to pay twice for kids to learn the same thing. Taxpayers shouldn't have to. I don't know University of Rhode Island's or Rhode Island College's remediation rates. It is 5 percent for Terrapins.

Robbing Peter to pay Paul has had tragic consequences. No one intended them. They are real with no obvious end. Kurt Vonnegut has a short story in *Welcome to the Monkey House*. Equality has become the law and is harshly enforced. Half the population has to wear devices that give them migraines.

Any high school graduate who wants to go to college should know enough to pass regular freshman courses. They haven't been able to for decades. Google *College and Career: Are Maryland Students Ready?* Here are the remediation scores for the same Blue Ribbon Maryland school: **60** percent of its high school graduates take remedial courses. **81** percent take remedial courses at their nearest community college.

You can see with these Maryland examples why my guess that other kids scored lower by at **1 to 2 percent** each year and was cumulative was not too far off.

I am well educated. I did a math proof in high school that got me scholarships. Oveta Culp Hobby—Secretary of Health, Education, and Welfare—chose me as one of 15 high school graduates in the nation to receive a full scholarship. The college received the same stipend as I did. Her assistant said I could now go to any college—just let them know. I graduated first in my college, was nominated for a Danforth, was full-time faculty at Johns Hopkins in psychiatry, recognized for my teaching, etc.

Ronald A. Wolk, who lives in Warwick, wrote my favorite book on public education: *Wasting Minds: Why Our Education System is Failing and What We Can Do About It*. Study this book. I have. Ronald Wolk succinctly discusses every issue but special education. Children in Finland, Poland, Singapore, Shanghai, South Korea, and other places learned more even as our children learned less.

Every factor Wolk discusses is important. I think teacher training is the most important. We would have more teachers except for the growth of "special needs" and IEPs. Again, my Blue Ribbon Maryland example shows how difficult and confusing it has been for parents and the public to keep track.

I have reviewed three reasons why I think my **1-2 percent** is right: 33 percent of New York City's budget goes to normal kids, low PARCC scores, and high remediation rates.

I think the best high school education process is Bob Lenz's *Transforming Schools: Using Project-Based Performance Assessment, and*

*Common Core Standard*s. Howard Gardner, at Harvard, is an education genius. My ideal high school content would include Howard Gardner's ideas on education, what is true (evolution), what is beautiful (Pachebel's *Canon*, Black Eyed Peas "I gotta feeling," *Hamilton*), and what is good (lessons from the Holocaust/Genocide in which 6 million Jews and millions of others were killed by Nazis and their collaborators during WWII, US slavery, American Indians). Wolk: "Research and experience should have convinced us by now that people learn best when they want to learn and when they confront problems out in the real world." Lenz and Gardner agree. I have many college examples myself. I think requiring statistics would help.

Kids with developing needs "versus" regular education have victims but no villains. We need tough love. Compassion and ignorance have led us astray: *"I am so sorry that your school-age child has such and such. In his/her case, all I am going to offer is the same opportunity, not more resources. Research shows the outcome you are asking and hoping for will be at another student's expense, who will learn less."* I am not critical of others who knew this and did not say anything. I haven't either.

Ideally, there would be a statewide meeting of hundreds of parents who think their kids have special needs and hundreds of parents who don't. They would examine the effects of my additive **1 to 2 percent** in Rhode Island. They would decide how the budget should be reallocated so that it now served the interests of all students. They would figure out how to make this happen and then implement it. They would measure the education improvement as they went along and make corrections as needed.

The above scenario is virtually impossible. I shall now give the only solution that has any real chance. I know Massachusetts parents with two normal kids in public school. They are desperately trying to get each child tested and given IEPs. They think their children will otherwise never be able to compete in life with the many kids who are going to better private schools. (A friend's child in New Jersey attends a private school whose tuition is $45,000 per semester.)

For months I thought what the Massachusetts parents were doing was wrong. I now think they have a brilliant solution that I was missing and can work for all public school children. Here is my recommendation. We should define all kids as "developing with special needs," and start all over. Education is in crisis. I see no other way.

Rebalancing regular students and "students with developing needs" will cause much public angst for two to three years and then be over. Do it for the children, all the children.

I like to quote experts or research. In this case, I can unfortunately quote myself.

Good luck, you'll need it.

Carl Young, PhD.

PART 3
CARL'S WISDOM

RETIREMENT THOUGHTS AND PATIENT ADVICE

No matter the problem, if it is big, no conventional solution is likely to solve it. Family therapists believe that interventions need to be at a level higher than the problem itself. My favorite example is of a Dark Ages walled city under siege. The enemy is hungry. Finally, just one day's worth of food is left in the city: a cow, a pig, some chickens, bread, etc. A wise person suggests that they throw all their food over the wall to the hungry outside, stand on the wall, and laugh. It works. The army fights over these items, thinks the siege is hopeless, and retreats.

Most change is just another variation of what the patient or corporation was already doing. The therapist behind the one-way window is more objective than the one in the room with the patient(s). Family therapists try to break the pattern of what is helping them.

Here is one intervention. I once worked with two other family therapists who were behind a one-way mirror. There was a phone in the room. "I am pretty sure that they would be calling in and saying that I was treating you like your former therapists and/or missing something big. I am going to wait before I say anything."

Marshall McLuhan popularized, "We don't know who discovered water, but it was most certainly not a fish." That is a good axiom.

It is difficult to stop bad habits. It is difficult to start good habits.

Maslow divided his five-level hierarchy into "being" needs (love and affection, self-esteem, and self-actualization) and "deficiency" needs (physiological needs and safety). Removing things that make people happy usually does not make them unhappy. Rather it results in the absence of feeling happy. Libraries, schools, and parks tend to make people happy. Most of the rest of our taxes go toward fire, police, roads, etc. We don't tend to feel happy when we get these later services.

The most powerful of all psychological findings is the law of effect. Anytime you do something and something positive happens, you are more likely to do that again. Positive reinforcement is the key. A very good book is Karen Pryor's *Don't Shoot the Dog! The New Art of Teaching and Training*.

A developmental model is the single best construct for understanding anything. You can no more escape its power than you can gravity. You need to work within it.

Jessie Barnard used to teach sociology at Penn State. She used this baseball analogy about relationships. First base is when we start off dependent on parents. Second base is a teenager's being counter-dependent. Third base is independence. Home plate is interdependent. She said that a very successful man is content with a pretty woman. A very successful woman prefers a successful man.

Staying current in one's field used to be more or less possible. It no longer is.

Scientific medicine should be legislated.

There are three types of health intervention—primary, secondary, and tertiary—that range from prevention to treatment.

There are three types of social interventions: power/coercive, rational/empirical, and normative/reeducation.

There are two types of errors: A type I error is detecting an effect that is not present. A type II error is failing to detect an effect that is present. You would rather a physician say you are sick when you are not, Type I, versus you are well when you are not, Type II.

I listened to a lecture by an adult learning specialist. He said that adults tend not to learn things in the usual linear fashion. They do things in fits and starts over time. It may take five or six attempts before they learn and act on it. It may take years.

Psychologists count three things: frequency, intensity, and duration.

Prochaska at the University of Rhode Island has made his version of "ready, set, go." He starts with precontemplation, then contemplation, preparation, action, and maintenance.

Tom Peters observed that with almost every commodity, Americans are willing to spend 30 percent more for real or perceived value. Americans are quite willing to spend more for auto upgrades from DX to LX or whatever. There is an interesting literature on the dissemination and utilization of scientific knowledge. For years, farmers preferred a weed treatment that killed the weeds over a product that kept weeds from growing.

One farmer told a county field agent to just stay in the car: "I already know how to farm better than I do."

The placebo effect (nonspecific) is so powerful that it is hard for any drug to beat it statistically. Expectation, conditioning, and meaning are powerful. Placebos are worth their own study. One wit said that he was addicted to placebos. He could give them up, but what difference would it make?

People learn better alone. They perform better in groups.

An "A" management team with a "B" plan usually outperforms a "B" management team with an "A" plan.

Thomas Paine: "What we obtain too cheaply we esteem too lightly. It is dearness only that gives everything its proper value." That would be cognitive dissonance. Men value their fraternities more when the razing/initiation is harder.

Never bet against human nature.

We have improved on Ruth's sickle but never on Ruth.

I once went to a conference that I had to drive 200 miles to get to and paid $400 to attend. It turned out to be worth every bit of effort and cost. I learned that if you keep using "and" and never use "but," you will have a strong interpersonal position that deflects negativity. You simply string together all the things you feel.

An axiom from *Getting to Yes* by Fisher and Ury is to be easy on people and hard on principle.

Carl Rogers was a famous therapist when I was in graduate school. He thought good therapy and relationships came from empathy, unconditional positive regard, and congruence.

During Japan's great financial run, Japanese corporations tended to spend 90 percent on defining the problem and 10 percent on solving it. American corporations tend to spend 10 percent on problem definition and 90 percent on solving it. I read that the appraised cost of everything in Tokyo is greater than that of all the United States.

People tend to have emotional set points. Neither negative nor positive situations tend to last as an influence. A lot of smaller positive things tend to influence us more than one large one.

My statistics professor said that over time anything that can happen will. Most things that we worry about that can happen are unlikely to happen.

When in doubt as a family therapist, prescribe the symptom.

Gazzaniga studied right and left brain phenomenon. His boss took credit for Gazzaniga's work and won a Nobel. Gazzaniga said that the brain has to interpret what is going on. The brain makes up stories that don't make sense. He feels this fact accounts for religion. It also accounts for pop-ins and lots of stuff.

White published *The Concept of Competence* in 1954 in which he argued that the zeitgeist explains success more than any great author does. Anytime you think you have a good idea so do dozens and maybe thousands of others.

Ernest Becker's *The Denial of Death* explains more behavior than most others. Skip his criticism of Freud because no one has that theoretical position anymore. Start with Otto Rank.

Freud said that neurosis is trying to solve in the present what only could have been solved in the past. If Freud's only contribution has been the concept of defenses, he would have still been a genius. "Man is the only animal that eats when he is not hungry and mates in all seasons."

I was sorry when neurosis was dropped as a diagnosis. I sued to tell patients that I had good news and bad news. The bad news was that they were neurotic. The good news was that there were only two other choices: psychotic or dead.

Howard Gardner said that there were eight kinds of intelligence: physical, musical, spatial, interpersonal, naturalist, logical, and linguistic.

George Vaillant says that the five more positive coping mechanisms are humor, anticipation, altruism, sublimation, and suppression.

The best general self-help book is Edmund J. Bourne's *Anxiety & Phobia Workbook*. I have the fifth edition.

I used to recommend Kevin Leman's *Have a New Kid by Friday: How to Change Your Child's Attitude & Behavior in 5 Days*.

I like Matthew McKay's *Couple Skills: Making Your Relationship Work*. His son was riding a bicycle in Oakland and yelled at a driver who was doing circles at a red light. Someone in the car shot him dead.

My favorite experiential book on pain is Reynolds Price's *A Whole New Life: An Illness and a Healing*. I gave it to a neighbor who is crippled from being hit by a car while walking her dog. She is in constant pain. She knocked on my door and said it had changed her life.

Risks do not add up. Advantages do not add up either. This is counterintuitive. Whatever one thing has the greatest probability will always be what accounts for it.

When I was a freshman in college, my bible professor, Ms. Stickland, told us the following about the Pentateuch. Something would happen that sounded bad. But, it turned out to be good. Then something happened that appeared good that turned out later to be something bad. These dazzling reversals happened repeatedly. She said, "Class, remember this. It is impossible to tell the difference between a blessing and a curse in the midst of it." Now I am an old man, and so it is.

You can never prove the null hypotheses. Research takes longer than it does.

Positive psychology has six components: wisdom and knowledge (creativity, curiosity, open-mindedness, love of learning), courage (bravery, persistence, integrity, vitality), humanity (love, kindness, social intelligence), justice (citizenship, fairness, leadership), temperance (forgiveness, humility, prudence, self-regulation), and transcendence (appreciation, hope, humor, spirituality).

Four types of equality: ability, opportunity, outcome, and resources.

Always ask for what you want.

There are many counterintuitive facts. Parents who are afraid of germs and clean everything with Lysol have sicker children.

No one ever went to their grave wishing they had worked harder for Blue Cross.

Not everyone bored is creative. Everyone creative was probably bored.

Your behavior speaks so loudly that I can't hear what you are saying.

There are no incurable diseases. There are incurable patients.

The founder of osteopathy said everyone's brain can write its own prescription. I read a book called *Write Your Own Placebo*.

Churchill: "I've always enjoyed learning things. I don't enjoy being taught."

Maturity is when your partner tells you to do something, you know it is the right thing to do, and you do it anyway.

It takes a very good man to beat no man.

Baldessarini: Psychiatrists in the US tend to try and maximize medicine's effects. Psychiatrists in Europe tend to try and minimize side effects.

Here is a scandal. ECT (electroconvulsive therapy) works 85 percent of the time as a first-line treatment for major depression. It works 80 percent of the time for treatment-resistant depression and bipolar disorder and sometimes schizophrenia. New magnetic treatment is available.

So far, I would rather be me alive than anyone I know dead.

I learned things from Daniel H. Pink's *Drive*: *The Surprising Truth About What Motivates Us.*

For reasons I won't go into, I am on the prepaid misery plan.

Here is a favorite quote about regret. Elvis said he made love to all his leading ladies but one. Someone asked Mary Tyler Moore if that were her. "What was I thinking!"

What the last white man hanged in Georgia said: "Except for the honor of it, I'd just as soon be somewhere else."

Man won't sign the United Way card. He is the only person in the company who won't. His supervisor cannot get him to. The manager cannot get him to. Finally the owner said that he would talk to him. The owner said you either sign that card, or you are fired. Guy goes back and signs the card. Supervisor asked him why. Guy said that no one had ever explained the United Way before.

P.T. Barnum: No one ever went broke underestimating the taste of the American people.

The reason there are stereotypes is because there are types.

Always get a second opinion. No one knows what he or she doesn't know.

"In the spring a young man's fancy lightly turns to thoughts of love." In the winter an old man's fancy heavily turns to thoughts of food.

Behind every liberated man is an exhausted woman.

Here is a story Dick Fisch told during my supervision: He had a patient whom he thought he'd probably helped more than anyone else. A couple of years later, he sees the guy in a mall. He asked his former patient how he was doing. The guy said life was one damn thing after another. Dick said that he was disappointed and told him why. The guy says that Dick had been wonderful. Before Dick, his life was the same damned old thing.

Keep your eyes open until you fall to sleep.

If you don't want to do something, do you want to want to do it?

Beard said that his multivolume history of the world could be summarized in these four quotes: When it is dark enough, you can see the stars. Whom the Gods would destroy they first make mad with power. The mills of God grind slowly, but they grind exceedingly small. The flower that a bee robs, it also fertilizes.

Instead of saying that I don't like something, I say, "I've never really learned to appreciate that" for everything from modern art to jazz.

There was nothing I ridiculed more in graduate school than this quote: "Behind every bent thought there is a bent molecule." Now I know that is true. I dread the day when I get a letter from Peabody saying that my degree has been rescinded for lack of quality control.

Here is a favorite cartoon. It shows a group of cavemen at the top of a high cliff. One caveman is being tossed off. The leader asks, "Is there anyone else who feels like their needs aren't being met?"

Hazel and Hobart have had a successful relationship for 35 years. Their secret? They are married to someone else.

ABOUT THE AUTHOR

 Carl Young graduated from Peabody College in Nashville, Tennessee in 1971. He had three major interests: clinical psychology, community psychology, and social psychology. He taught community psychology at Peabody, taught social justice in the Vanderbilt Nursing School, and did the same at Fisk University.

He also taught in the Johns Hopkins Department of Psychiatry, delivering a postdoctoral program in public psychology. He did research and taught organization development at the Homewood Campus.

Later he taught in the College of Human Development at Pennsylvania State University in State College. Carl's ethics course was required and included over 800 students. His graduate program was for mental health planning and development and was shared by the Community Development, Administration of Justice, and Health Planning and Development departments.

Carl worked for both Blue Cross and Blue Shield of Maryland and Rhode Island. He was licensed in five states and enjoyed a private practice.

Made in the USA
Middletown, DE
06 October 2022

12028903R00050